Classic SCHWINN Bicycles

William Love

WAM

books

First Published in 2003 by MBI Publishing Company, St. Paul, MN 55101 USA

Second Printing published in 2009 by WAM Books, Spokane, WA 99203 USA

Printed in United States of America

ISBN 978-0-615-28244-2

Edited by Amy Glaser
Designed by LeAnn Kuhlmann

On the front cover:
During the late 1930s, Autocycle was Schwinn's top-of-the-line model. This restored example shows off its desirable goods, including a cat's eye front fender "bomb," dual headlights, and a Stewart-Warner crossbar speedometer.

On the back cover:
Today, the ornament that adorns the front fender of this 1938 Deluxe Autocycle is called a fender bomb or a cat's eye. Originally, Schwinn referred to it as a, "bright metal safety ornament with an aerial bomb design."

(Bottom) Typhoons were top-selling middleweights from 1962 through 1982. The equipped versions had chrome fenders and rims. This Coppertone 1967 Deluxe also came with a three-speed hub, hand brakes, and whitewalls.

The author:
William Love collects and restores old Schwinn bicyles. His favorite pastime is travelling the country searching for and talking about the treasured relics.

Contents

Acknowledgments

I have never written an informational book without the generous help of others; this work is no exception. The large number of people involved in the bicycle hobby does not cease to amaze me, and their generous attitudes are equally impressive. I expect that there are helpful, caring people within all hobbies, but it would be difficult for them to exceed the level of willing cooperation that I have enjoyed from members of the bicycle hobby. Whether it was the sharing of literature, bicycles, or knowledge, I extend heartfelt thanks to all of you who assisted me with this project.

Special thanks are due to Leon Dixon, a longtime bicycle collector and curator of the National Bicycle History Archive of America. His bicycle interest goes way back, and his writings about bicycle collecting began over 20 years ago! Thanks to you, Leon, for sharing some of your vast knowledge and collection of data with me.

Dave Stromberger, who runs Dave's Vintage Bicycles, was also a valuable source of information to me. Stromberger's business involves the correct restoration of bicycles, and finding rare parts, so his database of knowledge (in his head and his computer) is vast. I truly appreciate your sharing this expertise with me, Dave.

Bob Ujszaszi (pronounced "u-SAW-zee") is famous for his restoration of vintage Schwinns and leather seats. He possesses not only a wealth of bicycle knowledge, but he also has a great collection of original vintage Schwinn classics. Thank you very much, Bob, for your help in getting photos of those old treasures.

Many other vintage bicycle collectors and enthusiasts were kind enough to share their knowledge and some of their bikes for photographs. I express thanks to all of you who helped in this way, and here you are in random order: Brett Sargent, Jim Houghton, Greg Bacha, Steve Warrington, Willard Stockton, Judy Fleming, Mike Carver, Kathy Bruce, Brian Franklin, Dave Gover, Mike Conley, Chris and Amber Smith, J. C. Reznikoff, Terry Morehouse, Dan Clark, Ian Ledlin, Joe Pleasants, Andy McCulla, Scott Boyd, Shawn Lefavour, Don Rohrer, Jeff Hensley, and Pete Aronson. You are all good people with some really great bikes!

Another thanks, of course, must go to my family for their sharing of me with the formation of this book. Thanks to my wife, Mary Ann, and to my son and daughter, Adam and Hilary, for your patience and support.

As usual, the MBI Publishing staff was helpful and expedient throughout the publishing process. Thanks to Amy Glaser and the rest of the editorial and design staff members who helped bring this book to your shelf. You all shine as individuals and as members of a very open, helpful team. Thanks to everyone involved.

Introduction

Beginning with the 1895 World Racer, the bicycles that Arnold, Schwinn & Company built were designed with pride and manufactured with a quest for high quality. Arnold, Schwinn & Company eventually backed this product philosophy with their lifetime warranty, and promoted a *Schwinn-Built* quality image throughout the latter half of the twentieth century. Through a mid-1960s name change to Schwinn Bicycle Company, and into a 1995 ownership change to Schwinn Cycling & Fitness, Inc., the company marketed multiple models and created countless classics. When a firm builds such a quality product, and when the product has an aesthetically appealing design and great functionality to boot, an object of timeless appeal is often the result: a *classic*.

Classic: It's one of those words that has definitions as varied as our fingerprints. We can find a basic dictionary definition that includes terms like "first class" and "highest

There is unanimous agreement that the Streamline Aerocycles are classic Schwinn bicycles. This 1935 model has plenty of classic criteria; many other Schwinns have less definitive classic status.

Cutoff years for classic Schwinns should not fall in the middle of production runs. Since the Sting-Ray series ran from 1963-1/2 through the 1970s, it would not be right to end the classic Sting-Ray category in 1965. The Pea Pickers were not introduced until 1969, and this nice 1972 example is certainly a classic Schwinn.

rank." Or we might give credence to another phrase from the dictionary definition that I prefer: something "of lasting significance or value." More definitively, as the term applies to bicycles, we must credit Leon Dixon, who wrote an article titled "Bicycle Classics" in the November 1979 *Bicycle Dealer Showcase* magazine. In that article, Dixon described the characteristics and classes of classic bicycles (single-tube, balloon, and middleweight) occurring in the 1920–1965 vintages. I generally agree with Dixon's guidelines, especially when it comes to the classic bicycles' criteria, which Dixon cites as having a certain styling, higher cost, presence of accessories, and, usually, a well-known manufacturer. I agree, and I wrote of similar classic, or collectible, criteria in the early chapters of my book, *How To Restore Your Collector Bicycle*. Regarding the year limits, however, Dixon is bound to get debate from the proud owner of a perfect 1971 Schwinn Typhoon Deluxe or the aficionado with a 1919 World Racer, both of whom might believe their bikes are classics. The upper-end year limit is the one that *I* believe should be broadened some; many of the classic bicycles made in the first half of the 1960s were still made virtually unaltered in the second half of the decade. From my observation, there are certainly models from the 1970s that warrant classic consideration, and as time continues, later decades will have their classic candidates.

In the specific case of classic Schwinn Bicycles, it's not natural to divide the Sting-Ray series in the midst of its model run, when they all seem to be classics. The point is that the term "classic" will always be used as an adjective (classic car, classic art, classic bicycle), or a plain old noun ("What a classic!"), when people describe something that appeals to them in some classic sense. Fine divisions are tough to enforce, since judgment is in the eyes of many beholders. Where opinions vary, disagreements are inevitable. Additionally, in the future, if not now, many owners of 1930s and 1940s bicycles will consider their bikes antiques, which are officially supposed to be from before 1920. Maybe classifications such as antique, collectible, contemporary, and classic need somewhat flexible bounds.

Old bicycles definitely had flexible manufacturing standards; there were often exceptions and inconsistencies in the bicyles produced. For example, it is sometimes difficult to say exactly when the production runs of certain models began and ended, because an exception that is one year earlier or later often appears. There are disparities of opinions over the exact year that serial number locations changed; which seat, handgrips or pedals were original; which rims were offered; and many other subjects of debate. These arguments are usually settled with a plus-or-minus-one-year approach. This approach is certainly used throughout this buyer's guide, because original bikes, expert opinions, and even factory literature reflect these ambiguities.

One fact to keep in mind is that the serial numbers on the frames designate the year of the frame production, and not necessarily the model year of the finished bicycle. The frame may have sat in the factory a year or more before it was assembled as a complete model. Additionally, many parts (e.g., spokes, pedals, seats, stems, rims) were purchased from outside suppliers, and these vendors were subject to change. If a parts supplier changed its product, or if Schwinn decided to buy from a different supplier, mid-year changes would take place without notice, as previous supplies were exhausted. This manifests itself in the marketplace where two bikes of the same year and model have different characteristics, or with the existence of an original Schwinn that the factory never made.

The early bicycle manufacturers were an independent lot. Even industry leaders like Arnold, Schwinn & Company were relatively small and under the control of only one or two individuals. This situation allowed flexibility, and sudden changes may have occurred due to materials availability or the whim of the company leader. Again, collectors who study such things all have tales depicting these inconsistencies—anomalies that add even more interest to the fascinating vintage bicycle hobby.

Bicycle dealers and owners also liked to customize their bikes. Because of interchangeable parts like rims, hubs, seats, pedals, handlebars, and accessories (tanks, racks, lights, etc.), many bikes were altered from factory stock when they were brand new. When such modifications were made with Schwinn parts from the same period, one might assume that the bike originally came that way from the factory. This is an example of why original documents or information from original owners is important in judging a bike as all-original or not, especially when evaluating a rare bicycle.

Serial numbers (like this one stamped under the bottom bracket) designate the year of the frame production. Keep in mind, however, that the model year of the finished bicycle may be a year later.

MBI Buyer's Guides for automobile and motorcycle marques depict various models with factory archive photos, and are able to relate annual production figures gleaned from factory records. For Schwinn bicycles, no such luxury exists. The archival material present at the factory was spread across the globe through a public auction in 1995. Well before that, in 1948, most of the early serial number records were destroyed in a factory office fire. Record keeping was better at Schwinn than at most bicycle factories, so at least some Schwinn serial numbers have traceable origins (see listings near the back of this book). Fortunately, Schwinn's potent marketing effort also left behind many sales brochures, dealer catalogues, and a lot of beautiful classic bicycles for us to study and enjoy.

One amazing characteristic of any classic artifact is its seemingly timeless appeal. Currently, in the instance of bicycles, not only do a wide range of bikes create classic interest, but a wide range of people (age, gender, background, etc.) are showing interest in classic design, quality, and corporate heritage as

Certain owners and dealers liked to customize their bikes. Accessories might match the vintage of the bicycle, but were not necessarily original equipment. For example, the airplane and the dual lights on this Aerocycle were not factory issue.

well. There are some themes common to classic objects of all types, regarding style, scarcity, durability, function, and others. Creating classics is not an ordered science though, but instead a wonderful blend of design, engineering, manufacturing, and marketing.

The best approach to the hobby of collecting something is to collect what you like. There are many guidelines presented here and elsewhere, but collecting is not an exact science; the bicycle hobby is most enjoyable when you deal with bicycles that have a certain aesthetic appeal to you. Whether it's one that you rode as a kid, envied at the kid-next-door's garage, or admired in the window of the bike shop, the appeal probably began a while back. Some of these classics are so appealing that one may fall in love even without a previous association. Again, look around a bit to find the classic bicycles that grab you for whatever reason, and you're sure to have some fun in the old bicycle hobby.

Ahead is an excursion through Schwinn's efforts, accomplishments, and the legacy of classic bicycles they created. These classic Schwinn bicycles, like bikes from countless makers, occupy a noteworthy position in the history of our nation, and they will be the objects of attention and desire for years to come. Let's see which ones pique your interest!

Star Rating Code

Rating anything in any category is inherently subjective, so it's no different for bicycle rating. Without a doubt, Leon Dixon (see Introduction) was right on the money when he included "a certain styling" and "the presence of accessories" as characteristics of classic bicycles. Dixon also included "expensive" in that definition, and for sure, the Schwinn classics leading the collector market were originally, and still are, expensive. However, many Schwinn models that were plain, economy models in their day, but have the right style (like a cantilever frame), are regarded and traded as classics today. This demonstrates that the many characteristics and variables that must be considered for rating the classic Schwinns will vary among the eyes of different beholders.

Another important difference between the classic definition followed by this book and that of Dixon has to do with time. The ratings here will not cut off the most recent classic bicycle year at 1965, as per Dixon. There are too many classic Schwinn models that continued after that year, like middleweights and Sting-Rays, to ignore them. There *was* a general fading of the classic Schwinns in the 1970s, although that is according to current thought. We should be open-minded to the idea that Schwinns from the 1970s and even later might be looked upon as classics in the future.

In the case of vintage Schwinns, some collectors think that all of them are classics. We shouldn't go *that* far, but just about each one has some degree of classic appeal. The star rating code stratifies the degree of classic appeal. Consider the ratings to represent a classicmeter for Schwinn bicycles. They will tell you how much classic clout the various models now have.

The models with the higher star ratings are generally rarer than those with lower ratings. As usual, however, with bicycles there is an exception to that: Sting-Rays. Sting-Rays and the offshoot Krate Series sold in record numbers, and are not that scarce today, but the current collector-clamor for them is huge.

The star ratings are not meant to be a value guide. Although the higher stars generally mean higher value, lower stars do not mean low value in every case. For example, the antique Schwinns, which have high value, do not have high classic status.

All of the Schwinns are durable and dependable, so they are not rated in those categories; they would all get four or five stars. They would all get a good rating for parts availability also; the parts that *are* getting scarce are even starting to be reproduced.

When the Schwinns receive their grades in Classic 101, here is what they will mean:

★★★★★ **Five Star Schwinns** embody and exemplify all of the classic traits: Top-of-the-line, fully equipped, new innovations, interesting classic style, unique or obscure feature(s), highest demand in the classic bicycle collector market.

★★★★ **Four Star Schwinns** have some of the classic traits: Good style and feature (equipment) level, good demand in the bicycle classic collector market.

★★★ **Three Star Schwinns** have good classic lineage (style) and some equipment. They have fair demand in the classic bicycle collector market, with potential to rise.

★★ **Two Star Schwinns** do not have special style or equipment, and are utilitarian in purpose. Demand is low in the classic bicycle collector market, with potential to rise.

★ **One Star Schwinns** are Schwinns all right, just not classic Schwinns. They have more function than style, and do not trade as classics in the collector market at this time.

Chapter 1

Identifying Old Schwinns

Arnold, Schwinn & Company, which became Schwinn Bicycle Company, and later Schwinn Cycling and Fitness (when sold to the Scott Sports Group and Chicago headquarters were vacated), will be referenced throughout this text simply as Schwinn. After all, regardless of the official corporate title or the various product nameplates, "Schwinn" is the name that we have associated with the company and their cool bicycles over the decades. It is also the name with marketing rights that sold in the fall of 2001 to Pacifica LLC (they market the Mongoose brand of bicycles) for many millions of dollars.

The vast majority of Schwinns that are worthy of the classic designation had their origin in the original Schwinn family-owned Chicago factory. The only arguable exceptions might be the factory Centennial reproductions (1995), along with the subsequent retro cruisers and reproduction Sting-Rays (1980s and 1990s). The owners of Schwinn during this recent reproduction and retro phase are no longer in the picture, so only time will tell what the new owners will do with the Schwinn brand name, and where their products will end up in the Schwinn classic heritage hierarchy.

Schwinn produced and marketed hundreds of models throughout the century between 1895 and 1995, and up until about a decade before their early 1990s failure, did

By 1898, "The World" cycles were Schwinn's mainstay. This early head badge depicts the logo: "The World." The cable address for Arnold, Schwinn & Company at this time was "Worldcycle."

a good job of satisfying the market's demands. It was, however, Schwinn's lack of a proper emphasis on the BMX and mountain bike market that led to their undoing. Nevertheless, early on (1895–1932) it was Schwinn's stronghold on the racing and adult market that gave them a sound foundation. The beautiful Schwinn models created during the next period (1933–1942) typified the "form follows function" theory of design: Create outstanding function and have faith that a pleasing form will ensue. These pre-World War II bikes, with some carryover art deco style, are some of the most sought-after classics among today's collectors. Later (1946–1973), with deluxe heavyweights, middleweights, and Sting-Rays, Schwinn would capture the youth market, eventually including the super-strong baby boomer group. Even Schwinn's counterattack to the imported lightweight bicycles created some of the solid old Schwinn models like the Racer, Breeze, Traveler, and Varsity that are on the plentiful and inexpensive end of the collector market scale today. As usual, though, there is an exception: Inexpensive, when it comes to lightweights doesn't apply to the Schwinn Paramount bicycles. The Paramounts have more of a racing origin than the mass-market lightweights; their top-quality components (like Campagnolo) and race-bred construction will assure these bikes a loyal collector base.

Let's review some of the Schwinn bicycle classifications mentioned so far. First, there are the early, early models (mainly racing and basic models) that are considered true antiques. Next are the adult bicycles of the 1920s. These bikes were still basic, but as they gained innovations like improved free-wheeling coaster brake hubs and accessories such as tanks, they made the a transition to the beautiful, stylish, well-accessorized, early balloon-tire bicycles (1933-1942). As these balloon-tire heavyweights took over the kid market after World War II, Schwinn could do no wrong in the marketplace, and followed up with a multitude of other models in middleweight, Sting-Ray, and lightweight versions. During this bicycle boom of the late 1950s through the 1960s, millions of classic Schwinns were produced, and the many examples remaining today fuel a growing following of fans.

There is more detailed information within the chapters that follow, but now is a good time to start learning some of the basic identifying characteristics of the various types and models. As mentioned in the introduction, absolute statements must be tempered with the reality that there may be an exception to any rule, and that even Schwinn company-produced documents contain some conflicting information. Also remember that classifications, categories, and cutoff years regarding style or type are subject to personal interpretation and preference. The divisions discussed here are mainly the ones that took place as the ever-changing market evolved.

After his early years in Germany as a bicycle designer and mechanic, Ignaz Schwinn decided to start his own enterprise. He came to Chicago during the World's Fair, and shortly after that, in 1895, incorporated Arnold, Schwinn & Company with a partner, Adolph Arnold. A bank president, Arnold no doubt was an asset in obtaining startup funds, but Schwinn was the bicycle expert. Schwinn designed the product and the tools to make it, selected machinery and equipment, hired the personnel, and set up a bicycle factory in Chicago. By 1908, Schwinn had purchased the interests of his partner and become the sole owner of Arnold, Schwinn & Company.

Ignaz Schwinn's ambition was to produce the finest bicycles in the world. Around 1884 an Englishman named Starley had invented the Safety bicycle design, which was to compete with the contemporary high-wheel bicycle. The Safety had the configuration of two smaller, same-sized wheels, so a rider didn't fall as far during a mishap.

Near the end of the nineteenth century, Schwinn established a strong reputation in bicycle racing. In 1899, Charles M. Murphy rode behind a train at a speed just over 60 miles per hour. Events like this brought a lot of attention to Schwinn bicycles.

Schwinn was convinced that this design, with its pneumatic tires, chain drive, and lower rider position, represented the bike of the future. This instinct was correct, as the Safety was the basis for Schwinn's success; with some refinements, it is the same bicycle we use today.

Schwinn's first model, dubbed the Standard Roadster, had a simple diamond-shaped frame, without fenders or chain guard, and a weight of only 19 pounds. The tires were a 28-inch glue-on single-tube design, in which the tube and tire were an integral unit, as opposed to the later tube-in-tire setup. For the company's first 20 years, this basic design was the staple of the model lineup. Variations in frame bar positions were about the only model differentiations.

By 1898, the "World" cycles had become Schwinn's main product identity; in fact, their cable address at the time was "Worldcycle." The World models were of a basic design and suitable for racing. Bicycle racing was popular around the turn of the century, and Schwinn used this venue to popularize its bikes. During this time, Schwinn bicycles had more official victories than any other company's bikes. In 1899, Charles "Mile-a-Minute" Murphy was the first man to be clocked at 60 miles per hour on a bicycle, which he accomplished on a Schwinn World Racer. This phenomenon was the type of event that made for invaluable advertising in those times. The sales booklets of that era touted the Schwinns as "the best medium-priced wheels."

Through the 1910s and 1920s, these basic models filled Schwinn's lineup, although some 24-inch and 26-inch tire models were added to the 28-inch line. Also as a result of team racing, tandems, quads, and even five-man quints were built in the Schwinn factory. Most of these early, antique bicycles will have "The World" imprinted on the head badge, along with the glue-on tire-and-rim setup. These early bicycles are referred to as classic Schwinns by many people; this is hard to argue, and they *are* very valuable, but some of the models that came later seem to possess even more inherent classicness.

Schwinn purchased the Excelsior Motorcycle Company in 1911 and bought the Henderson Motorcycle Company in 1917. Schwinn's Motorbike model (it had no motor) of 1922 showed some motorcycle influence, such as an add-on tank, and was described in sales literature as having "no equal in appearance and equipment." This would be the turning point in a trend toward heavier, accessorized, loaded bicycles. Schwinn continued to identify itself not only

Introducing the balloon tire to American bicycles in 1933 was one of the most significant events that Schwinn ever initiated. It was the platform for a myriad of upcoming innovations.

Shortly after the balloon tire made its debut, well-accessorized or equipped bicycles became popular. The 1936 Autocycle was a formidable representative for Schwinn in this new class of bicycles.

with motorcycles, but with automobiles and airplanes as well. The company offered the Auto-Bike in the mid-1920s, and would sell the Cycleplane, the Autocycle, and the Aerocycle in the 1930s—all confirmed classics.

In 1930, Schwinn created a new department combining bicycle and motorcycle engineers. Their task was simple: improve quality and appearance. The motivation for this move was that Ignaz Schwinn, and to an even greater extent, son Frank W. Schwinn (then age 36) wanted their bikes to be the standard of quality and innovation for the industry. The first 30 years of Schwinn bicycles had undergone only minor changes that were mainly in the style category. Functional innovations were the next order of business, and a new tire that Frank W. Schwinn had seen in Germany would lead the quest. This tire was an automobile-type double-tube, or tube-in-tire design called the balloon tire, and was introduced on a Schwinn bicycle in 1933. This tire held up longer, was easier to repair, rode softer, and would help introduce the next era of streamlined and deluxe bicycles.

In bicycle vernacular, there would now be equipped and unequipped bicycles from which to choose. They could also be categorized as loaded versus plain, or deluxe as opposed to standard. The equipped, loaded, or deluxe models carried accessories like tanks, horns, lights, racks, mechanical innovations (spring forks, expander brakes, and other special features), extra chrome, and

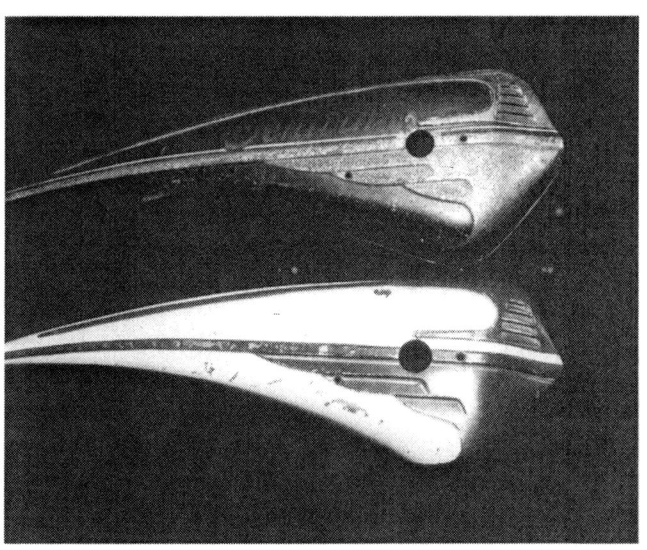

Tanks, like these from a Phantom (top) and a B-6 (bottom), were designed to fit below the top frame tube. Many tanks had a built-in horn, like the versions shown here. The large hole is for a horn button. This is the type of accessory that appeared on the equipped models.

more. The unequipped, plain, or standard models lacked some of these niceties, but were built just as well as the fancy models. Some collectors actually prefer the unequipped versions. All of these terms will be used throughout this text to classify the trim levels of the various classic Schwinns.

Many different varieties of lights adorned the equipped bicycles. A popular brand that Schwinn used on their bikes was Delta. This Delta Rocket Ray is from a Schwinn Panther.

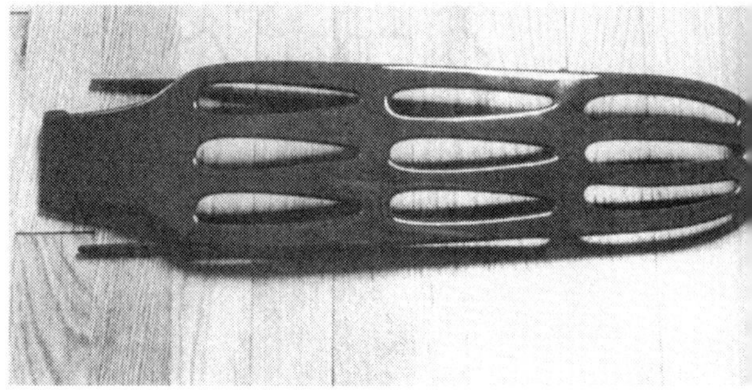

Racks or carriers were often part of an equipped bicycle's accessory list. For an obvious reason, this one is referred to as Schwinn's nine-hole rear rack. Schwinns sported many versions of front and rear racks over the years.

During the 1930s, Schwinn introduced other mechanical innovations like the Forewheel (front) expander (drum) brake and the knee-action spring fork. Some trendsetting style showed up too, especially in models like the Aerocycle, which premiered in 1934. The deluxe Schwinn models from this period were heavily equipped with lights, racks, horns, speedometers, and premium saddles, and stood out from their predecessors because of it. The full-fendered streamlining of these models, along with their sturdy balloon tires, many accessories, and art deco styling make them standouts in the classic arena.

Schwinn's patented knee-action spring fork was introduced in 1938. It was a simple design, but added a lot to a bicycle's appearance and ride. Today it adds greatly to the classic appeal of any bicycle so equipped.

The now-famous cantilever frame first appeared on the 1938 Autocycle. The Autocycle bicycles had it all when it came to extras. The model seen here can be identified as a 1938 because of the upward angle of the lower rear fender braces (they are nearly level on 1939 and later models).

Bikes of the 1930s were starting to appeal to the nation's youth market, because of improved ride and eye-appeal. Schwinn had been trying to appeal to kids since around 1919, as adults were turning their attention to cars. Whether by skill or accidental luck, Schwinn bicycles of the next 40 to 50 years would definitely appeal to kids, which accounted for Schwinn's sales dominance during this time. The baby boom after World War II would be responsible for unprecedented sales centered mainly on the youth market.

Per Frank W. Schwinn's wish, his company produced some very lavish models during the decade preceding World War II. The innovations in function and style firmly set the pattern for Schwinn's success in the coming years. The introduction of the Aerocycle, Deluxe Autocycle (with the now-famous cantilever frame in 1938), and the Deluxe Cycleplane (Motorbike), brought us beautiful classic styles, along with a long list of features. Some of these obscure features, like the cat's eye fender "bomb" or the crossbar illuminated speedometer, are just about too cool for words, and virtually assured the initial and future demand for the bicycles they adorned. This tendency toward unique style and function did not end here.

After World War II, Schwinn wasted no time tweaking its model lineup. Beginning immediately with the 1946 models, the now-legendary built-in kickstand, then called a parking stand, was offered. The semi-tubular

The Streamline Aerocycle (1934–1936) set Schwinn's standard for streamlining and accessorizing in its era. This and other equipped Schwinns from this period now set the standards for the most sought-after classic Schwinns.

In the one-of-a-kind department, the Autocycle speedometer is hard to beat. Obscure items like this alloy-housed, illuminated speedometer really add to a bicycle's classic appeal and value.

Speaking of obscure items, this cat's eye fender bomb holds a prominent position on the front fender and on the list of not-so-ordinary bike accessories. A bright lime-green reflector-glass in a stylish alloy mounting enhances the classic status of this 1938 Autocycle.

fender braces were improved in 1946 and were used for the next 40 years or so. Another small innovation designed at this time and used for years to come was the detachable seatpost clamp with a special shaped, self-locking bolt head. These items, along with popular pre-war features (spring fork, cycle lock, expander brakes, etc.),

Some Schwinn-patented innovations were subtle, like the detachable seatpost clamp with a self-locking bolt head (1946). Although minor in comparison to inventions like the cantilever frame, the new seat clamp applied even tension around the post and avoided excessive bolt stress.

were to be a large part of Schwinn's identity in the future.

By the end of the 1940s, the popularity of the loaded, super-deluxe bicycles reached a crescendo. The announcement of the Black Phantom in 1949 brought to market what was arguably the ultimate heavyweight. This bicycle was designed to be the object of desire for every kid in America. It had all the extras, and a black, red, and ivory paint scheme that commanded attention in dealers' showrooms and on the street. With its striking colors, horn-tank, lights, racks, and 2.125-inch whitewall Typhoon Cord tires, it really was a beautiful creation, and a future classic.

Beginning with the Phantom, each Schwinn Bicycle would derive its identity from a pool filled with a wealth of upcoming

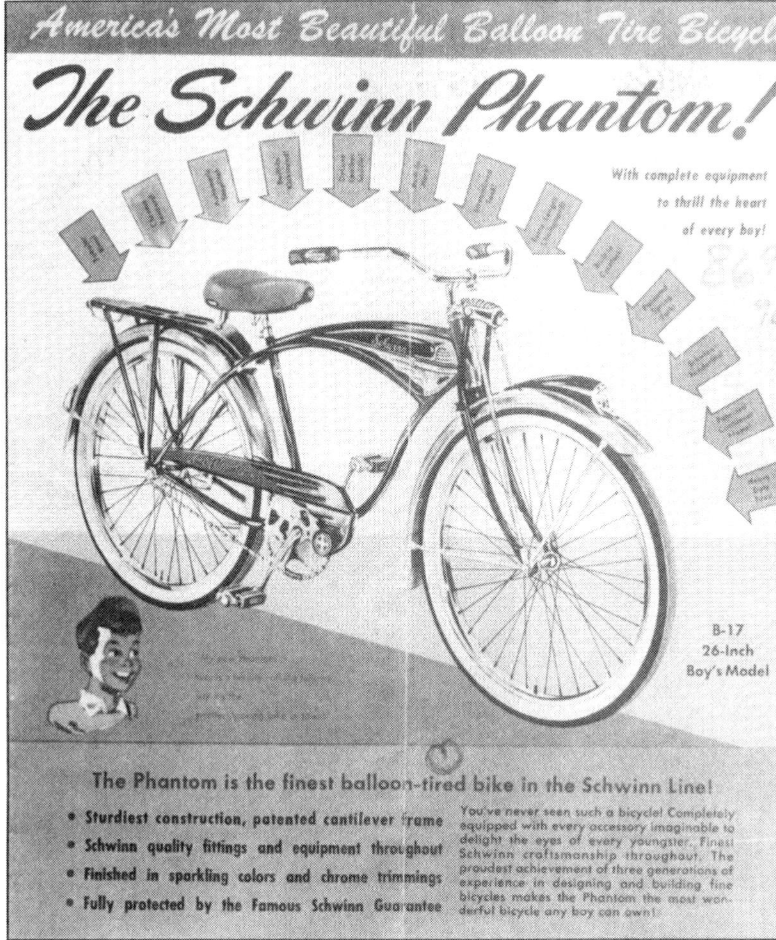

The Black Phantom is considered by many to be the consummate classic from Schwinn. It became extra-popular because it was timed nicely with the baby boom after World War II. Introduced in 1949, it included all of the popular equipment that was conceived over the previous decade-and-a-half.

Below: Model names began appearing on the chain guards in about 1949, with the introduction of the Black Phantom. From then on, numerous names appeared on millions of Schwinns over the next 50 years; Spitfire is just one example.

model names. In the 1950s, new models such as the Panther, Hornet, Starlet, and Spitfire had their names proudly displayed on the chain guard. These model names, each with its own logotype, were present along with other "Schwinn" identification on the frame tubes, tanks, and head badges. The earlier bikes with model names, like Aerocycle, Autocycle, and Motorbike, had their names on the tanks, but the no-tank bikes usually displayed their name on the head badge only.

An increased emphasis on a "Schwinn-built" identity to the bicycles was now gaining strength. Most of the names that *did* appear on a Schwinn bike prior to World War II were anything but "Schwinn." Names such

The Schwinn name began to dominate the head badges after World War II, but there were still many varieties. A stylish and popular version is this "planes, trains, and automobiles" badge used on a 1948 D model.

Prior to World War II, there were many names emblazoned on Schwinn head badges. Packard was one of the several names, as were Liberty, Admiral, Pullman, and Majestic.

as Liberty, Admiral, Pullman, Majestic, Packard, and Ranger are some of the brand identifiers that are present on frame-tube decals and head badges of those old bikes. This was because other companies distributed Schwinn-built bikes, and those companies chose which name they wanted on the product. Even Schwinn seemed unwilling to promote its own name for many years, as the early head badge identifications that Schwinn used read "World," "Excelsior," or "Excelsior-Henderson." Evidently, by the 1950s the Schwinn brand had a good enough reputation to stand on its own, and a bike with a Schwinn name was a positive sales point. This fact, coupled with the strength of the growing Schwinn dealer network, eliminated the need for distributors, finally allowing the bikes to be identified as Schwinns. The exception to this is that a fair number of bikes were sold through retail tire stores, with the B. F.

Left: The Excelsior name was used frequently on Schwinns up until about 1950. There were several designs which used both the Schwinn and Excelsior names, such as this stylish example on a 1950 Phantom.

Below left: "X" marks the spot on this late 1930s head badge design. Later, the Schwinn name would dominate the head badges.

Below: Finally, after the use of many other names, this mid-1950s head badge is all Schwinn.

B. F. Goodrich was still selling Schwinns into the 1960s, but the oval shape was now linked to Schwinn. Even though B. F. Goodrich got top billing, note the words "Schwinn-Built" at the bottom of the badge.

Goodrich name, from the late 1940s to the early 1960s.

The curb jumping heavyweight Schwinns were selling well in the 1950s, but the lighter, sportier, imported bikes were making their way to our shores in increasing numbers. Schwinn's lightweight models weren't lightweight or stylish enough to directly compete with these imports, so Schwinn needed another alternative for the potential buyer. The solution was to build a bike with a lighter, sportier design than the heavyweight balloon-tire models, but with the same durability. The imports did not have a reputation of holding up well under rough use, a factor that was used against them in the Schwinn showrooms. Hence, the middleweight era began with the introduction of the Schwinn Corvette in 1954. This was not only a lighter bike than the previous design,

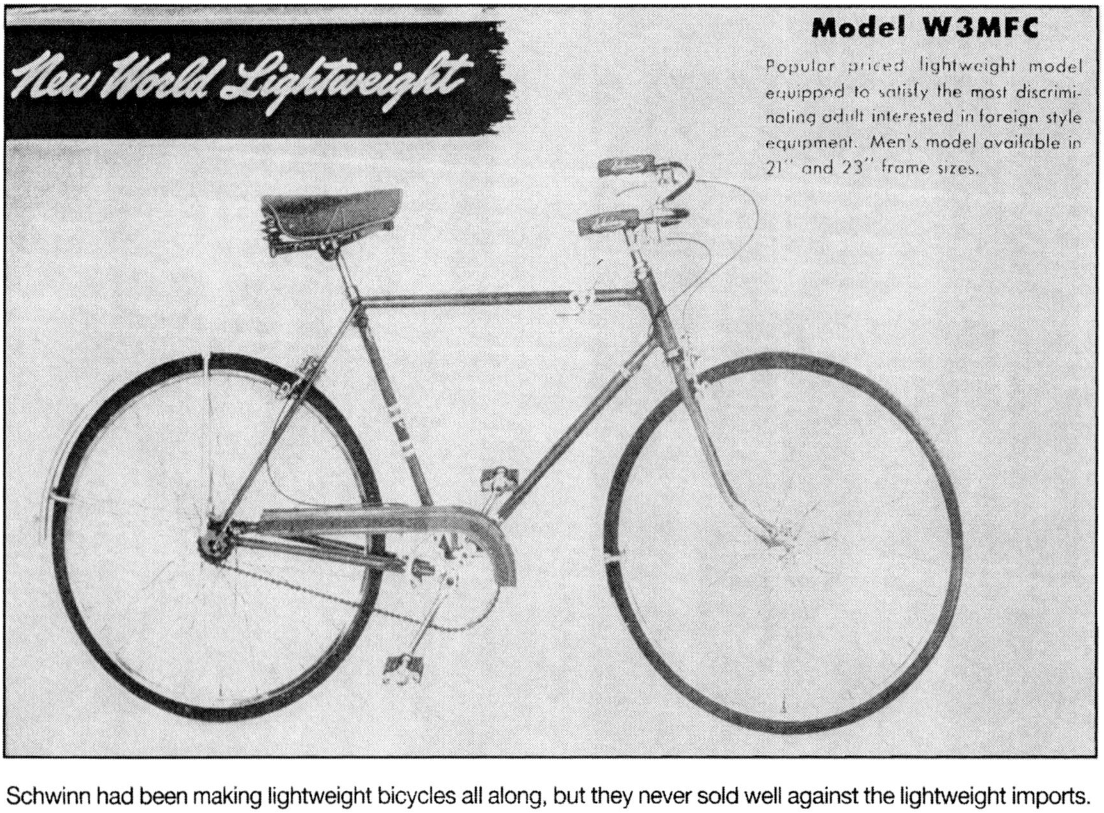

New World Lightweight

Model W3MFC

Popular priced lightweight model equipped to satisfy the most discriminating adult interested in foreign style equipment. Men's model available in 21" and 23" frame sizes.

Schwinn had been making lightweight bicycles all along, but they never sold well against the lightweight imports.

A line of middleweight models was a compromise between balloon-tire heavyweights and lightweights. The middleweights commenced in 1954, and were similar to the heavyweights, but had narrower tires. This 1960 Speedster is typical of the middleweight models.

it also had narrower tires, and could be equipped with an import-like shifter and hand-operated caliper brakes—components that actually *were* imported.

Another market change that began to take place in the 1950s was an increased offering of girls' bikes, along with more 20-inch and 24-inch models. The full-sized 26-inch bikes still posted the strongest sales, but the baby-boomer kid market was getting so vast that there were plenty of buyers of all sizes, and certainly in both genders. Schwinn had some ladies and juvenile models way back in the 1920s, but not nearly the lineup that was offered to these market segments from the 1950s to the 1970s.

It must be mentioned that girls' bikes are generally less desirable than the corresponding boys' bikes in the collector market. This mainly has to do with the concessions made in the girls' frame designs to accommodate the "step-through" feature. It must also be stated that Schwinn produced a lot of unique girls' bikes with classic designs and features, and they should not be overlooked as collectible treasures. The good news is

Schwinn offered an increased number of girls' bicycle models through the 1950s and 1960s. As you can see in this comparison, though, the girl's bike on the left doesn't have the same classic look as the boy's version because of the difference in frame designs.

that the girls' bikes are more affordable than the boys' counterparts today, and they are usually found in better condition than male-owned examples.

The middleweight line of bicycles was Schwinn's bread and butter for the next couple of decades (1955-1974), but right in the middle of their run another phenomenon came to market: the muscle bike. Schwinn introduced its Sting-Ray muscle bike in the middle of 1963, and made chopper versions dubbed the Krate series in 1968. This model took the youth market by storm, and in fact, it was the youth that started the trend. Dealers in California reported to Schwinn that they were selling a lot of 20-inch bikes, which kids were modifying with polo seats (also called banana seats), and high-rise handlebars (also called ape hanger, butterfly, and longhorn bars). Schwinn marketing man Al Fritz took this information to heart and pushed the Sting-Ray (which Fritz named) through development and into production.

Actually, the first Sting-Rays are identified as half-year introductory models, or as 1963–1/2. The introductory model was very basic but sporty, akin to the muscle cars of the period. This new 20-inch model was promoted to the public as easy to ride, easy to balance, and easy to pedal. The Sting-Ray was promoted to the dealers as easy to sell. It was probably *buying* by the public, rather than *selling* by dealers, that fueled this fad, however, and the fad was not fleeting. About 45,000 Sting-Rays were sold in that first half-year, which was about twice as many as Fritz

Schwinn introduced its legendary line of muscle bikes in 1963–1/2. The early models were very basic, without fenders. This example sports a dealer-installed spring fork, which was introduced (for Sting-Rays) on the 1965 Super Deluxe Sting-Rays, and used later (1968–1973) on the Krate series.

predicted, and about four times more than the next best selling model. The Sting-Ray line expanded, and sold successfully over the next dozen years (1964–1975), until its popularity gave way to BMX bikes.

The expansion of the Sting-Ray line included the typical deluxe and girls' models, but the biggest hit was the Krate series. These specialized muscle bikes had a smaller, 16-inch tire on the front, for the dragster look. Further dragstrip influence was evident in the rear slick tire and the car-like stick shift. The shifter controlled a freewheeling rear derailleur, so this "hotrod" also needed hand-operated caliper brakes—even a disc brake by 1972. To add even more to the custom appearance, Schwinn's patented spring fork suspension of 1938 was modified and placed up front. The Krates had a lot of appeal then, and still do today, as their current values rival those of much older, more rare Schwinns. In fact, the Krates are one of the few exceptions to the general rule that high-value collectibles have low availability; there are still plenty of Krates and other Sting-Rays to be found.

So, the antiques (1895-1919), the 1920s bikes (which slowly evolved to the 1933 balloon-tire models), the balloon-tire heavyweights of 1933-1964 (including the loaded deluxe models from 1934-1959), middleweights (1954-1983), and Sting-Rays (1963-1980) have all had their mention. Many of these models are certainly worthy of the classic designation, and they will be described with more detail in the chapters ahead.

The least classic of this listing is the antique group, not strictly because of Leon Dixon's category designations (see Introduction), but because these bikes simply didn't possess the level of classic design and features that the later models did. The antiques will still have their own chapter, however, because of their historical significance, scarcity, demand, and high value. Also, there are some people who will argue that these antique bikes are indeed classics.

Three final Schwinn classifications are Special models (Cycle-Truck, Whizzer, tandem, and three-wheeler); reproductions and current model cruisers; and lightweight models. That first category (special models) certainly has many classics within it, and has its own chapter ahead. The recent reproductions of the Black Phantom and certain Sting-Ray models may be loosely defined as classics (they *are* replicas of classics), so they will be discussed because they give credence to the impact of the original versions. The current retro cruiser models, which mimic older designs (and therefore have a classic appearance), also have a chapter, as do the lightweight models. Even though Schwinn made lightweight (narrow tire) designs through much of their history, they have a much lower current demand than other old Schwinns, probably due to the lack of style

The rear axle dropout slots on Schwinns produced through 1945 are rear-facing (shown on the frame at lower right). On the 1946 and later bicycles, they are forward-facing; they look like a hook.

Most balloon-tire Schwinns before 1948 used the drop-center rims shown here. There were some flat, Lobdell-brand rims used in the 1940s (see Chapter 3).

and accessories. Schwinn lightweights, especially their lightweight leader, Paramount, are well-built and stylish bikes, no doubt. Unfortunately, the average lightweight model is not yet considered classic, and the Paramount probably fits better into a vintage racing category. Schwinn lightweights are good bikes that may see increased classic popularity in the future, and should be viewed as up-and-coming collectibles right now. As time passes and other models become harder to find, lightweight models will surely be more noticed.

Finally, some random production facts and characteristics will assist you in identifying old Schwinns, so here are a few to consider. The cantilever frame design began in 1938. Up until 1945, the rear axle dropout slots on Schwinns had rear-facing slot openings, which became front-facing slot openings starting with 1946 models. The first year for a built-in (as opposed to bolted-on) kickstand was 1946. Schwinn tubular S-2 rims replaced the drop-center style in 1948; the 1948 rims had no center knurling, while the 1949 and later rims had center knurling. Serial numbers were stamped under the bottom bracket (crank hanger) until 1952, when they were moved to a left rear axle dropout location. In 1970, the serial numbers were stamped on the head tube, below the head badge; this was a mid-year change, so 1970 frames have

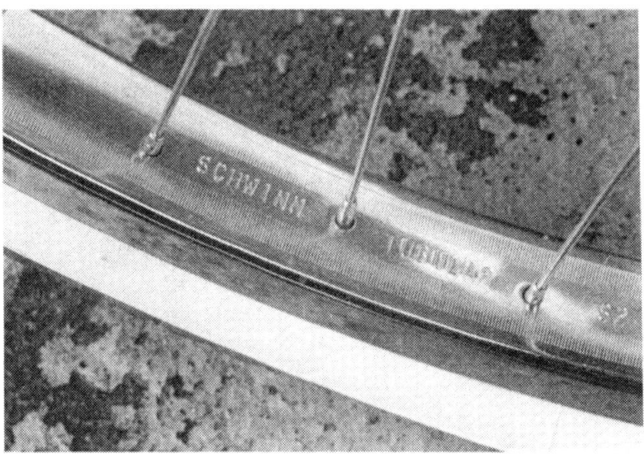

In 1948, Schwinn produced its own rim, dubbed the tubular S-2. The 1948 versions were smooth, but 1949 and later S-2 rims are knurled (the small lines), as shown here.

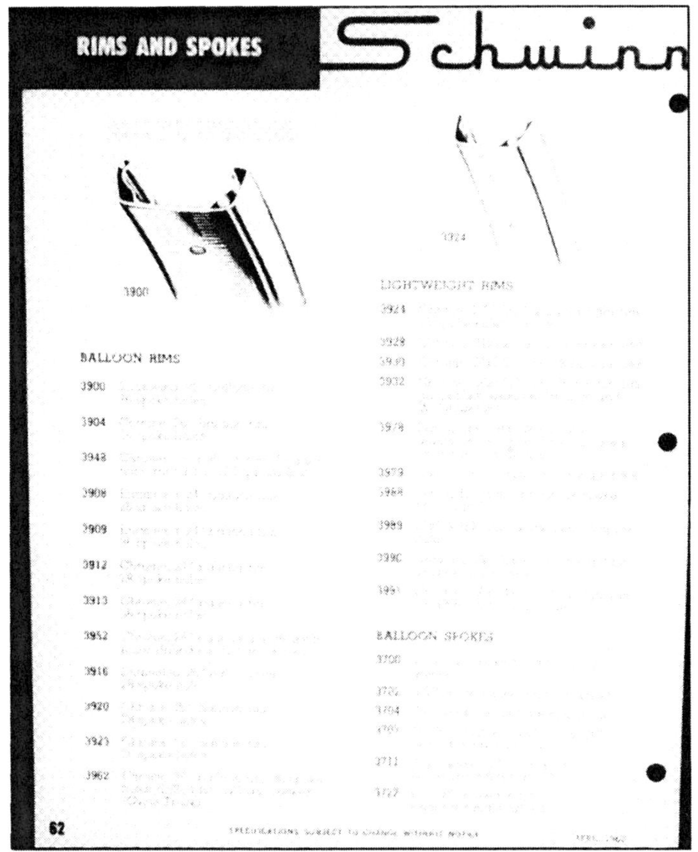

RIMS AND SPOKES

Schwinn

BALLOON RIMS

3900

3904

3948

3908

3909

3912

3913

3952

3916

3920

3923

3962

LIGHTWEIGHT RIMS

3924

3928

3932

3978

3979

3988

3989

3990

3991

BALLOON SPOKES

3700

3702

3704

3711

3722

62

By tubular, Schwinn meant that the rim was formed from a crushed tube (as shown in cross-section), a design concept that made for a very sturdy rim.

Above: The cantilever frame, which began in 1938, had to be one of Schwinn's top creations. Here appearing on a 1968 Typhoon middleweight, this frame design was used on heavyweights, middleweights, and Sting-Rays.

Left: Early Schwinn serial number stampings through March 1952 appear on the underside of the crank hanger (bottom bracket).

numbers in both places. The date that the pedal crank was produced is usually cast into the crank on the portion that rests in the bottom bracket (you have to remove the crank to see it). The Sturmey-Archer three-speed hubs have their production year inscribed on the external housing. Schwinn used a plastic head badge with a decorative Starburst design on some models in 1961 and 1962. These and other identifying characteristics

From April 1952 through early 1970, the serial numbers are stamped on the frame near the left rear axle dropout; they can be in either place in 1970.

Below left: A good place to find a clue to the year of some Schwinns is on the crank casting. The crank must be removed to do this, but the year is shown in two-digit format: 61 or 1961 in this example. If the crank is original, this number is usually close to the year of the bike.

Early in 1970, the serial number location moved to this head tube location, below the head badge.

will be discussed within the model chapters to follow, so this is just a sampling.

Now you have a general knowledge of the Schwinn bicycle models produced through the company's classic-bearing years. The following chapters will supply more details to aid in spotting and buying these vintage treasures. Enjoy those old Schwinns!

The Schwinns equipped with Sturmey-Archer three-speed rear hubs offer another method for their dating. The year of manufacture is stamped on the housing: 68 or 1968 in this example.

In 1961 and 1962, Schwinn used a decorative Starburst badge on some models. This type of badge is plastic and is glued (as opposed to screwed) on.

Chapter 2

★ Antique Schwinns 1895–1932

Antique Schwinns

The word *classic* is intentionally absent from this chapter heading. From 1895 through the 1920s, Schwinn's bicycles (and those of other manufacturers) lacked the style, the popular innovations, and the accessories to embody the feel of what most consider to be a classic American bicycle. This in no way minimizes the historical significance of this period of bicycles, during which Americans were introduced to two-wheeled self-powered transit. In fact, in dollar value, documented antique Schwinn bicycles in good condition outdistance the best of the popular, classic Schwinns.

The 1895 World Roadster is based on the simple diamond frame. Unfortunately, due to standardization and industry complacency, a 1925 vintage Schwinn looks just about the same.

All bicycle collectors admire the antique bicycles, but since there are so few of these original old bikes remaining, they cannot be in the collecting mainstream. Additionally, no American bicycles aroused much excitement before 1930; they were mostly plain, and all looked pretty much alike, making it difficult to tell them apart. In Schwinn's own history book, published in 1945, it was admitted that if the bicycle had anything in the way of an outstanding characteristic from 1900 to 1932, it was monotony. Besides the boredom of so little model differentiation, antique bicycles are even harder to identify now that they are about 100 years old.

Any of these remaining important and valuable antique bicycles should certainly be preserved, as with the many that are now protected in museums and in the hands of serious collectors. Without a documented history, though, and with so many manufacturers of bicycles at the time, it is extremely difficult to impossible to verify specific makes and models of the various antique bicycles. Again, their numbers are so few that the average collector will never see one for sale.

The historical importance of these first Schwinns is inarguable; however, so a little history of them is in order. A look at history will show what events prepared Schwinn for, and led them to, the production of so many classic bicycles.

In 1895, when Arnold, Schwinn & Company began, the hands-on partner, Ignaz Schwinn, already had experience as a bicycle designer. He also fully understood the importance of dependability and durability to his product, and how to achieve it. This quest for quality was the foundation and legacy of Schwinn bicycles. As one of the few companies to emerge and prosper out of the thousands of bicycle manufacturers in existence at the start of the twentieth century,

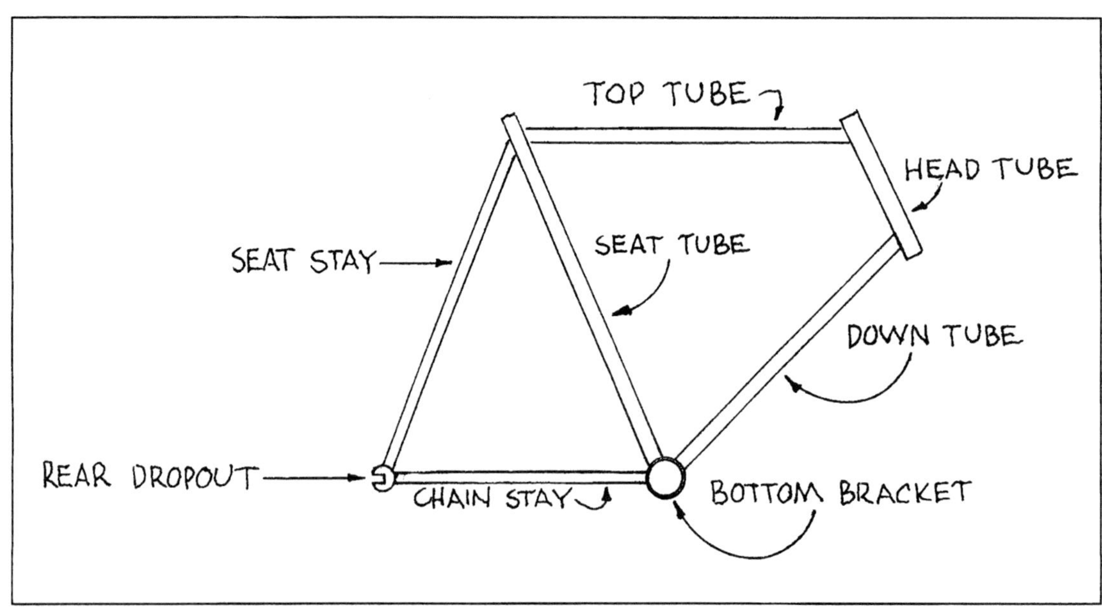

The antique Schwinns used simple diamond frames. The designation is derived from the diamond shape that is formed by the top tube, down tube, chain stays, and seat stays. The points of the diamond shape are the head tube, the seat, the bottom bracket, and the rear dropout. This functional design is still used today, but it does not rank well in regard to classic style.

Schwinn had more going for itself than luck. By the time Ignaz Schwinn took over sole ownership of the company in 1908, Schwinn bicycles had proved their quality with more racing victories than any other maker. These were glorious formative times for Schwinn.

At the same time bicycles were gaining in popularity, however, there was a new mode of transportation making big waves: the automobile. It didn't destroy the bicycle industry, but it sure put manufacturers in a quandary. How could they sell bicycles to adults who could now buy a used car for less money? With the existing bicycle line, it would be very difficult. During the 1910s and 1920s, good bicycles were priced around $100, and used autos were available for $30 to $50. In 1900, American bicycle industry sales were over one million units, but in 1904 the number sold fell to around 250,000. This harsh reality influenced the eventual lowering of bicycle prices and the emergence of new models. To succeed, the bicycle had to become appealing for adult recreation as well as transportation. That task was going to be an uphill battle, so makers would also have to open up the child market.

Prior to the concerted effort to improve Schwinn bicycle quality and design after

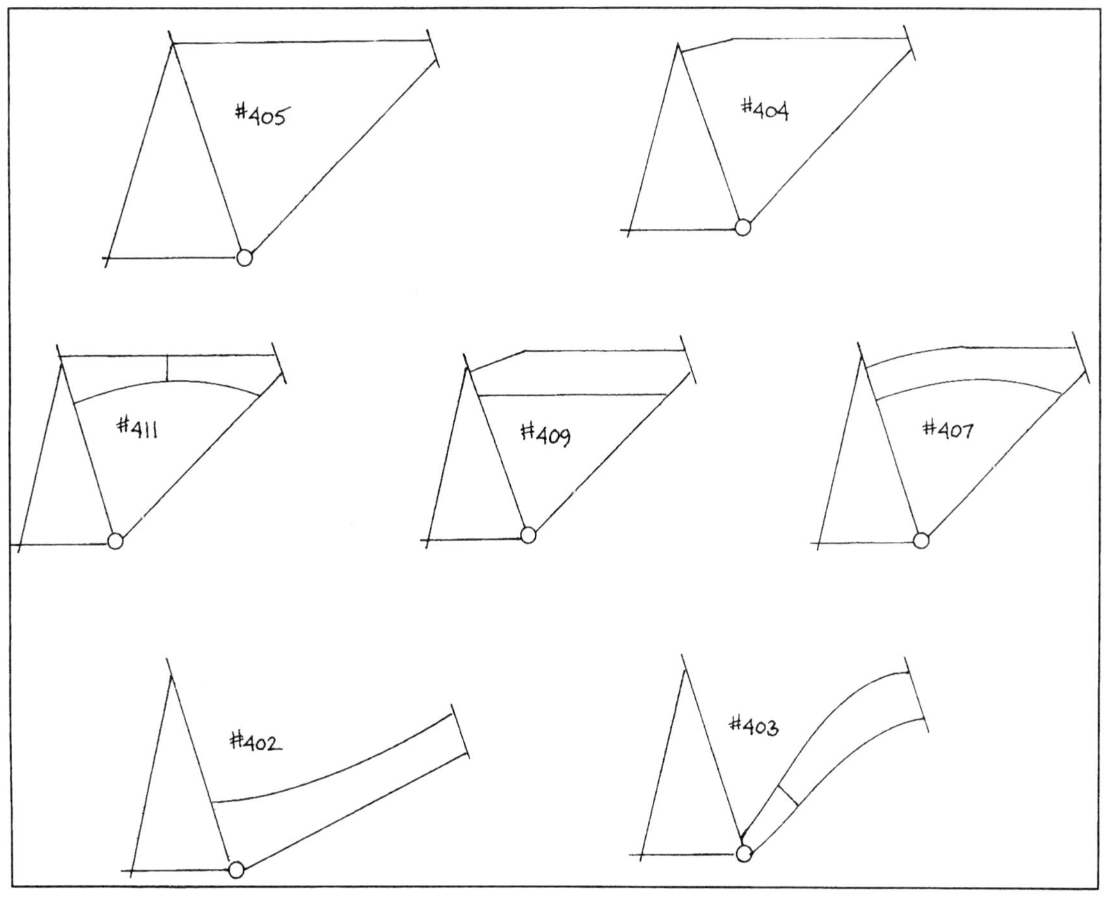

There were some variations made to the basic diamond frame design by the mid-1920s. Adding curves and new angles would be the key to creating more appeal and classic lines, as some of these early Schwinn frame designs show.

The 1895 World Racer was of the same typical design as every other bicycle of the time, and almost every bicycle for the next 25 years. Note the lower handlebars that are used to achieve the racing body position.

1930, Schwinn models were pretty basic. They all had the simple diamond frames, where a diamond shape was formed by the top tube, down tube, chain stays (the tubes running from the crank to the rear axle), and the seat stays (the tubes running from the seat to the rear axle); the points of the diamond shape were the head tube, the seat, the crank, and the rear axle. Until the more stylized frames began to appear in the late 1920s, the only frame variations for Schwinns were those with an extra bar or two welded within the diamond-shaped frame.

The sameness of bicycles built during this period had to do with the standardization that was taking place within the industry to bring down prices. In 1947, reflecting on pre-1930 bicycle designs, Frank W. Schwinn, son of Ignaz, wrote, "The stupid policy of standardization and stuffiness which the industry pursued for over 30 years had held it back." There was no excitement generated by new models, because they were just like the old ones. It took a factory expert to tell one make from another, because most of the parts were shared among makes, and every cycle shop had its own name badge. During this period, Schwinn stocked over 220 different nameplates for its customers. In 1930, Frank W. Schwinn would proclaim a mandate to remedy this sad state of the industry (see next chapter).

Even though these bikes were not very exciting at the time, and they are not true classics, they are important and valuable relics of bicycle history. The first bicycles from Schwinn were The World series in 1895. There was a Roadster, a Racer, and even a ladies' model with a step-through frame produced. But they *were* just bicycles in their

By the end of the antique bicycle era, style and accessories were creeping in. The presence of mud guards (fenders), tanks, racks, lights, and horns was foreshadowing the period of classic bicycles and innovations that was about to arrive. In its resolve to build better bicycles, Schwinn would produce a lot of classics in the coming years.

simplest form: no mud guards (fenders), no chain guard, and no accessories. In 1898, Schwinn offered the model 48 and model 49 as the "Best Medium Priced Wheels," according to their catalog. By 1922, there were some hints of flexibility, as the lineup included a 24-inch boys' model (number zero), along with model numbers 1, 2, 3, 4, 5, 7, 9, 10, and 11. They must have been superstitious about 6 and 8. Now there were actually some fenders showing up on the bikes, along with a top-bar hanging tank (tool carrier) on model number 10. The standard bikes used 28-inch diameter tires at this time.

In the 1920s there were about 10 model numbers in the lineup, but they were still all fundamentally the same: sturdy, but angular and unattractive bicycles. Schwinn did not enjoy strong brand recognition at this point, because the bikes continued to be sold with nameplates like World, Excelsior, Henderson, Admiral, Pullman, Majestic, Packard, Liberty, Ranger, Electric, and many others. Only manufacturers with assets and expertise would survive this period, but they would also need a new approach to do so. That approach would mainly be to make bicycles affordable and appealing to America's youth. The existing product line was not accomplishing that, and Schwinn needed to do—and soon would do—something about it. It's too bad that more of these antique Schwinns did not survive over the last century. As a result of time, two world wars, a depression, and early apathy toward bicycles, these old bicycles undoubtedly hit scrap piles by the tens of thousands. The ones that are left must certainly be protected and cherished, along with the many classic Schwinns that followed these antique treasures.

Chapter 3

Classic Heavyweight Schwinns

★★★★★	Aerocycle
★★★★★	Cycleplane/Motorbike
★★★★★	Autocycle 1936–1941
★★★★	Autocycle 1946 and later
★★★★	Phantom
★★★★	Panther (boys')
★★★	Phantom (girls')
★★★★	Jaguar
★★★	Hollywood
★★★	Starlet
★★★	Other boys' heavyweights
★★	Other girls' heavyweights

The heavyweight, or balloon-tire Schwinn bicycles are the most classic of the classic Schwinns. They were designed in response to Frank W. Schwinn's 1930 mandate to improve the quality and appearance of Schwinn bicycles. There had been very few changes made to

This 1939 Autocycle Deluxe carries most of the innovations from the previous few years. The Cycelock (1936), the Full-Floating saddle (1936), the Fore-wheel brake (1937), the spring fork (1938), and the cantilever frame (1938) all create classic clout. Niceties like the fender torpedo, dual headlights, and illuminated speedometer add even more character. Bikes like this are the pinnacles of classic Schwinns.

Schwinns—or any bicycles—over the previous three decades, but the proliferation of models to come would change that. Beginning with the 1933 introduction of the balloon tire (2.125-inch), the character of the Schwinn bicycle leapt out of the doldrums regarding innovation and style.

Balloon tires were an automobile-type tube-in-tire design that had not been used on American bicycles prior to 1933. With its American introduction by Schwinn, the new tire was called a double-tube design, because it replaced the old single-tube setup where the tire and tube were one, and glued to the rim. The new balloon tire gave a superior ride, was easier to change and patch, and, as Schwinn stated in its product information literature, represented "A construction embodying all the latest advancements in the tire art." Before long, bicycles from all makers would use these tires, which had the same design as the tires still used on bikes today.

The first balloon-tire Schwinns were identified by model numbers instead of names. The 1933 catalog listed the B10E men's equipped model, and the lesser equipped B9 and B4. The ladies' offerings were the B3 and B1–1/2. For the next couple of years, there were also models with the old single-tube 1–1/2 inch tires, which were simply designated model numbers 1, 2, 3, 4, 5, and 9. By 1936, only the juvenile Schwinn bicycles had the old 1 1/2-inch tires, and by 1937, every model except the lightweight racers carried the 2.125-inch (2–1/8) balloon tires. It's interesting that before World War II, the models were designated men's and ladies', and after the war the model reference of boys' and girls' became the norm. Also beginning about that time was the use of names for the various bicycle models rather than just numbers.

The balloon tire served as a new platform on which to build bicycles with a plethora of new features and accessories. Besides affording the new models a sturdier appearance, the low-pressure balloon-tire gave the bikes a more pleasant, softer ride. Within a few years of the balloon-tire introduction, classic features were rolling out of the Schwinn factory at a fast and furious pace. Features like the Fore-Wheel expander brake (1937), the Cycelock (1937), the spring suspension fork (1938), and the cantilever frame (1938), are all prominent classic bicycle features.

The cantilever frame was probably the most significant style feature that would affect the image of millions of classic Schwinns. The timeless style of this frame is one of those rare items with practically universal appeal. The cantilever frame was used on heavyweights, middleweights, Sting-Rays, Cruisers, and BMX bicycles. Isn't imitation considered the sincerest form of flattery? If that is so, the current makers of beach cruisers and custom bikes, who mimic

This is a rarely seen straight-back Cycelock attached to a 1936 Autocycle. Very few of these were produced before the design changed to an angled key position.

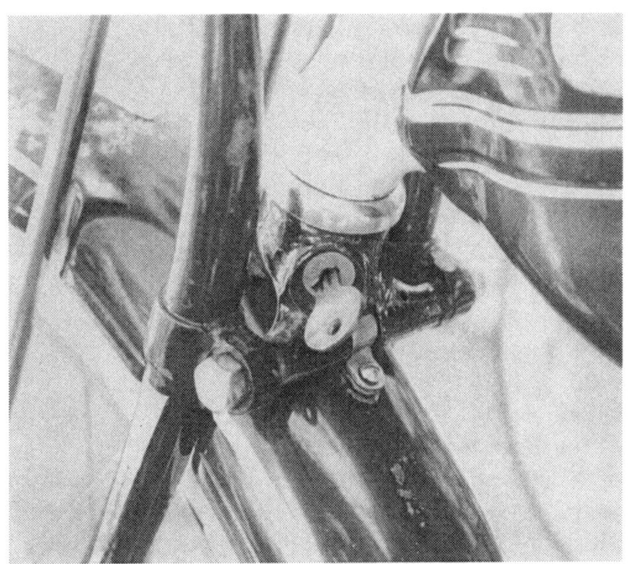

The Cycelock that most are familiar with is the New-Angle Cycelock, as Schwinn introduced it in 1937. The angled position offered improved ease of use, and the lock remained in this position throughout production.

the design of the cantilever frame in their products, are flattering Schwinn in the process. Apparently the patent rights have expired now, unlike in 1948, when the Whizzer Company tried to copy the cantilever design, and Schwinn promptly threatened a lawsuit. That skirmish actually led to an agreeable joint effort between the two companies, where Schwinn's frames were used on most Whizzers, a motorized bike. A Whizzer executive, Ray Burch, also came to work for Schwinn's marketing department in 1948. Burch honed Schwinn's dealer network during the 1950s to the "Total Concept Stores" that the company was touting. This marketing concept, which eliminated Schwinn sales by dime and hardware stores, barbers, taverns, and other less-than-expert outlets, was another big factor in the quality image that Schwinn portrayed.

It's not just features, frame designs, and dealer images that create classic bicycles; the form and function of the total assembly must pass scrutiny over time to gain classic status. When it comes to Schwinn bicycles, successful examples of this great mix of metal, rubber, paint, chrome, plastic, leather, and marketing are plentiful. In its resolve to build better bicycles, Schwinn produced a lot of noteworthy heavyweight classics. These cool bicycles are still around today in fairly large numbers; let's take a look at some of the coolest ones.

Aerocycle

The aviation industry was growing by leaps and bounds in 1934, so associating a product image with airplanes was probably a good idea. For conveyances like bicycles, even though they didn't actually fly, this association lent the exciting images of speed, freedom, and cutting-edge technology. For the

The Aerocycles kicked off a new era for streamlined, equipped bicycles. If you couldn't see this silver and red 1935 model coming at you with its aero-type fuselage and light leading the way, you might get a blast from the EA Lab Siren (horn).

It's amazing what balloon tires, a rear carrier, chrome, stylish fenders, and a custom tank can do for a bicycle's image. The Aerocycle started a new trend at Schwinn emphasizing style and innovation.

Aerocycle, Schwinn was not coy about this product identification; they placed a big airplane graphic on the tank, and claimed in ads that the new welded frame was "built like an aeroplane fuselage."

The complete model name for this newly stylized classic was the Streamline Aerocycle. Streamlining was a prominent design element for many items in the 1930s. Streamlining airplanes helped them fly better and faster, so such designs started there, but automobiles, motorcycles, and even appliances were getting their corners and sharp edges rounded off during this period. Schwinn jumped on this styling bandwagon with the 1934 introduction of its flagship model: the Streamline Aerocycle.

The Aerocycle sported the newly introduced balloon tires, and was equipped with

This Aerocycle's molded glass headlamp lens and its winged bezel represent the kind of unique detail that exemplifies classic design.

If the name and tank design were not enough to associate the Aerocycle with flight, Schwinn affixed this cool graphic to the tank to perpetuate the image.

an all-new, streamlined, teardrop-shaped tank. The tank was reminiscent of an airplane fuselage, and housed compartment for tools, battery, horn, and headlight. In keeping with the aero theme, there were wings cast in the bezel surrounding the headlight. The most common paint scheme appearing on Aerocycles was silver and red. In fact, according to Schwinn advertising, the only color combination available was aluminum (silver) and red. In this format, the tank and fenders were silver; the frame and tank/fender graphic accents were red. Color combinations of black and ivory, maroon and ivory, blue and ivory, and orange and black can be seen on original bikes today, however, reinforcing the concept that in the case of Schwinns, there are often exceptions to the rules. Any Aerocycle is rare and desirable, but those having color combinations other than silver and red are even scarcer and more coveted. The Aerocycles all came with single-speed coaster brake hubs, but the wealth was shared among the brake manufacturers New Departure, Morrow, and Musselman. The rear rack was promoted as a luggage carrier in the original advertising literature; they must have traveled light back then.

The Aerocycle was sold for the model years 1934, 1935, and 1936. Pinning down the exact year of an Aerocycle (like all Schwinns prior to 1948), is difficult, due primarily to the destruction of records during a factory fire in 1948. The serial numbers are stamped under the bottom bracket (crank hanger tube), but no official reference lists exist. Many times, thanks to original paperwork, specific features, or owner recollection, the actual year of a certain bicycle is known. Collectors compare serial numbers of bikes with known vintages to approximate the era of a given frame. In the case of the Aerocycle, the 1934 and 1935 frames are identical, and the 1936 frame has built-in fork stops to keep the fork from hitting the tank when the wheel is turned extreme left

This is not a reflector situated on the rear fender; it is actually an electrical taillight (note the wire under the light). The criss-cross Schwinn logo is molded into the red glass lens—a rare part.

Even the housing for the rear taillight is a heavy-duty, two-piece, solid steel, chromed assembly, and is an intricate detail on its own.

or right. Also, if the crank is original, the model year of the bike is cast on the pedal crank. This number appears on most Schwinn cranks on the portion that sits inside of the crank hanger.

Besides the streamlined look, there are other features responsible for the Aerocycle's classic status. The one-of-a-kind taillight was a certain classic creator, with its chrome housing and a lens featuring the word *Schwinn* molded twice in a horizontal/vertical criss-cross pattern. The large horn, by EA Laboratories (the Gangway brand was also used), was a stylish chrome masterpiece prominently mounted atop the handlebars. Everything about this classic-styling trendsetter appeared new and different. While it was widely agreed that the Aerocycle was a desirable bicycle, it was not a best seller, due most likely to its high price. Schwinn had the style and feature categories satisfied, but they needed similar appeal at a more affordable price.

Cycleplane/Motorbike

Schwinn had all of the bases covered with its new-for-1935 model 35. It had plenty of equipment, a lower price than the Aerocycle, and a name that brought forth images of cars, airplanes, and motorcycles. The catalog listing called this new model a Cycleplane, but the bicycle had "Motorbike" emblazoned on the tank. There was no motor, just the reference to one. The Cycleplane (Motorbike) came in equipped and unequipped versions, and was available for the model years of 1935 through 1939.

This 1935 Model 35 Deluxe appeared in dealer catalogs as a Cycleplane, but the identification on the tank was always Motorbike. The most common reference used for all of these models is Motorbike. For the final year of production, 1939, even Schwinn dropped the Cycleplane designation from its promotional material.

The following excerpts from a 1935 product catalog exemplify Schwinn's pride in this exciting new model:

> Frame—Double bar with unparalleled beauty and strength. Tires 26 x 2 –1/8-inch Cord Balloon. Tank—A new wider, rounder tank, which gives the low sweeping lines of a motorcycle design. Ample room for tool storage and clips for holding battery. Saddle—Padded bucket type. Handlebars—Chromium braced, with large rubber grips. Pedals—Highest grade, rubber. Guards [fenders]—Streamlined automobile type, enameled to match and beautifully striped. Rims—Deep drop center, chromium finish. Coaster Brake—New Departure, Morrow or Musselman. Chain and Guard—Chain of highest grade. Guard is chromium plated. Does away with any danger of accident to fingers or clothing in the sprockets or chain. Luggage Carrier—Welded steel, special design. Electrical Equipment—Beautiful new chromium plated headlight and horn. The headlight switch is conveniently located on top of the tank and the horn button on the right handlebar. Color—black with ivory trim, standard. Optional, red with ivory trim.

It's easy to tell from that catalog copy that Schwinn was excited about the beauty and features of their new bike. The Deluxe Cycleplane, or Motorbike, would remain about the same during its three model years, except that the frame down tube (from the head tube to the bottom bracket) was curved on the 1937 model; it had been straight in 1935 and 1936. The Fore-Wheel brake and the Cycelock were available for the first time on the 1937 models also.

The Fore-Wheel expander brake definitely grew from Schwinn's ownership of the Excelsior and Henderson motorcycle companies. It featured automotive-type internal expanding brake shoes activated via a hand lever and cable. This brake was somewhat over-engineered for mere bicycle use, but it sure looked cool, and was certainly a classic

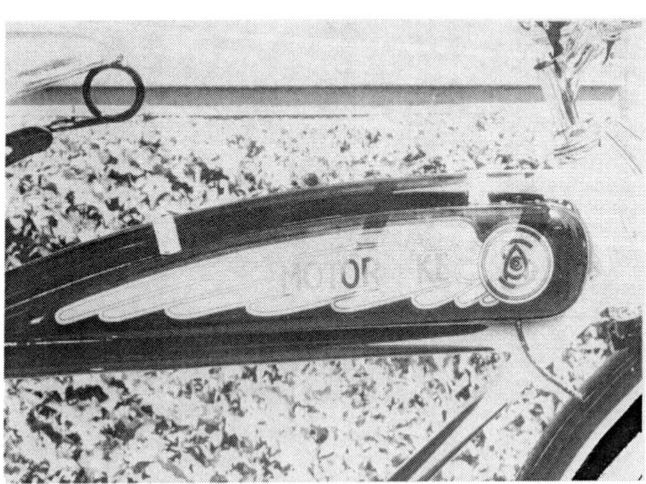

The new double-bar frame made a perfect mounting spot for this Motorbike tank. The tank was designed to hold tools and batteries. This 1935 model tank was plain at the front, as were the 1936 models; 1937 and later Motorbike tanks had small louvers at the front.

The Delta Gangway horn was mounted to all Deluxe Motorbikes. It was battery powered, and activated from a handlebar-mounted switch.

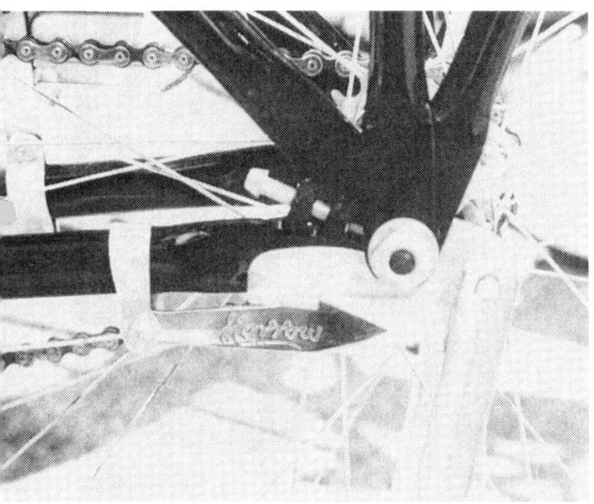

New Departure, Musselman, and Morrow were all listed in the catalog as available brands for Motorbike coaster brakes. This 1935 Motorbike sports the Morrow, considered by many to be the best of the three choices for design and durability.

Schwinn used many badges on their early balloon bikes. This "The World" version is one of the most popular with collectors today. This perfect example adorns the head tube of a 1935 Motorbike.

As usual, Delta was Schwinn's factory-installed brand of choice for headlights. The Delta light atop the front fender of this 1935 Deluxe Motorbike was original equipment.

feature. Schwinn's information sheet for the dealers promised, "The greatest sales booster since our introduction of the balloon tire. Velvety smooth braking or instantaneous stop in emergency. It will sell more bicycles for you." The Fore-Wheel brake was available on all 24- and 26-inch balloon-tire models.

Schwinn touted the Cycelock as the "final solution of the bicycle theft problem." The Cycelock was a Yale lock built into the front fork crown that locked the fork and front wheel at such an angle that the bicycle could not be ridden or wheeled. This feature was introduced in late 1936, and was revised to the new-angle Cycelock in 1937. In the first version, the key pointed straight back when the wheel was straight, and the new design had the key at an angle to the side. Schwinn even offered theft insurance for its bikes that

This 1939 Motorbike carries some of the subtle changes that took place since 1935: The Fore-Wheel brake (available in 1937 and later), a curve in the down tube (began in 1937), and louvers at the front of the tank (1937 and after).

were Cycelock-equipped. The Cycelocks on Cycleplanes and other models were examples of the many small features that added classic character to these old bikes.

The Motorbikes were available, as usual, in men's and ladies' varieties, equipped and unequipped styles, and in smaller juvenile versions. Like all Schwinns at this time, head badge identification could be any one of many possibilities. Names such as Excelsior, World, Majestic, Ranger, and Liberty are just a few of the many badges used. Since the

Some changes are very subtle as years pass by. The lens for the front fender light on this 1939 Motorbike differs from the 1935 model; it now looks more like an automobile headlight lens.

Cycleplanes/Motorbikes were all produced prior to World War II, they employed rear-facing axle dropouts for the rear wheel; after the War, the dropout slots faced forward. These bicycles epitom ized and kicked off the mass-produced classic bicycles that Schwinn would continue to make for years to come. They could be called very early "classic cruisers," a title that Schwinn applied to the actual cruiser models 50 years later.

Autocycle

So far, there was clear identification of Schwinn bicycle models with airplanes and motorcycles, but only hints of automobile association. The year 1936 was the time to take care of that, with the introduction of the Autocycle. Schwinn dealer literature pronounced that the Autocycle was "The Bicycle Sensation of America." It was one of the most stylish, well-equipped bikes on the market when it was introduced; it would get even better with the advent of the Fore-Wheel brake, the spring fork suspension, and the cantilever frame, all due within a year or two.

The first Autocycle had some unique new features. The tank sported small louvers at the front, and Stimsonite reflectors on

This 1938 Autocycle was restored by Bob Ujszaszi, and is representative of the 1936 introductory Autocycles that brought the curved down tube to the double-bar frame. This is a rare, fully equipped 1938 version with the double-bar frame, because the New Autocycle with a cantilever frame came out the same year. Both types were offered in 1938.

The cantilever frame models dominated the Autocycle lineup after 1938. This 1941 Super Deluxe Special was marketed under the Henderson name, even though it's all Schwinn. The tank design is exclusive to 1941, and resembles the later Phantom-style tank. *Bob Ujszaszi*

both sides (now called a jeweled tank). There was a new front fender accessory called the safety fender ornament, which was described in the catalog as a "Bright metal, aerial bomb design, with high power reflective button." These very stylish, alloy reflectors are now referred to as fender bombs, or cat's-eye reflectors. Their heavy, teardrop-shaped casting is classic in character for sure. As long as Schwinn was making cool aluminum alloy castings, they decided to make a classic speedometer. Easily one of the most significant

The cantilever frame created a space with a new shape for the tank. This 1940 tank is hard to find, because 1940 is the only year of the Autocycle to have the horn button located on the tank. Other years have interchangeable tanks. *Bob Ujszaszi*

This introductory model 1936 Autocycle has a lot of equipment, but is a bit too early to have a Fore-Wheel brake or a spring fork. *Bob Ujszaszi*

bicycle accessories ever, the large, streamlined speedo-meter housing covered the full width of the handlebars and was attached near the grips. The speedometer head resided within the center of the long housing and was illuminated. This was no ordinary speedometer; it had a Bakelite button at each end by the handlebars, one to light up the speedo face, and one to honk the electric horn. Today, the fender bomb and the speedometer have a great deal of value all by themselves.

The fender braces were flat for the last time on this 1936 Autocycle. Beginning the following year, they had a semi-tubular design. Some of the lower models used up Schwinn's remaining stock of flat braces over the next couple of years. *Bob Ujszaszi*

Top: The double adjustable stem for the Autocycle was described by Schwinn as "unbreakable." This one has lasted over 60 years so far.

Above: The Full-Floating leather saddle had a coil spring within the seatpost to give the rider a suspended ride.

As the years passed, Autocycles continued to be the top-of-the-line Schwinns. They were stunning bicycles, available in maroon, blue, or black, with ivory trim, and in two-tone brown or two-tone green. Besides the many features that they had in the beginning, the Autocycles received the flurry of innovations that continued coming over the next several years. Features like the cantilever frame (1938), the spring fork (1938), the streamlined fender light (introduced in 1941 and later used on the Phantom), semi-tubular fender braces (1937), and the built-in kickstand (1946) all had roles in keeping the Autocycle at the forefront of American bicycles. First, the top model was the Autocycle (1936 and 1937), then the Autocycle Deluxe (1938 and 1939), and finally the Autocycle Super Deluxe Special, which made its debut in 1940.

As you might guess, the Autocycle Super Deluxe Special had it all, with features like the newer (1938) cantilever frame, spring fork suspension, expander brakes both fore and aft, and whitewall tires (then called black and white). All of these goodies

Top: Visible here are some of the features that destined the Autocycle to become a classic Schwinn in the ultimate sense: dual Seiss headlights, jeweled tank with reflector, and a fender ornament that Schwinn described as "Bright metal, aerial bomb design, with high power reflective button."

Middle: The cast housing for this Autocycle's illuminated speedometer is quite a marvel of design by itself. Many parts used on Schwinns were made by other companies, like this speedometer head made by Stewart-Warner.

Bottom: EA Laboratories supplied electrical components to Schwinn; this Bakelite horn button is an example of their products. The speedometer illuminates when you push this button. Wires were mostly concealed by routing them into holes drilled in the handlebars.

were in addition to the long list of other Autocycle features. Generally, the unequipped Autocycle had no tank or headlight. The standard Autocycle had the tank, but only one headlight, no speedometer, and no fender bomb. And the deluxe Autocycle had a speedometer, twin headlights, and the fender bomb. When the Super Deluxe Special came about, all that was left to add were the dual expander brakes and whitewall tires.

The Autocycle series lasted until 1949, so these classic treasures ended up in the hands of many happy cyclists during the model run. Because of wartime restrictions on consumer

Top left: The year 1938 was the first for the chromed feather chain guard, which is proper for this 1938 Autocycle.

Left: Since the built-in Schwinn kickstand did not appear until 1946, this 1938 Autocycle used a Miller brand bolt-on-type stand.

Above: The Fore-Wheel front brake on this 1938 Autocycle is properly restored. Often, restorers will chrome the brake backing plate and actuating lever, which the Schwinn factory did not do.

Schwinn used what they called in 1936 literature the "famous" Stimsonite 3-inch reflector on the rear fender of the Autocycles.

products, there were only a few basic Schwinns made during the years 1942 through 1945. Beginning in 1946, the "Autocycle" name did not appear on the bicycles, which were then called B6 models. During the postwar baby boom, the kid market was expanding rapidly, and Schwinn was eager to capitalize on that. If you look at the Autocycle models closely, especially the models after 1940 with the streamlined front fender light, you will see hints of the upcoming Phantom series. The Autocycles embodied most of the innovations that the Schwinn style and quality task force came up with during their intentional,

Above: This reflector, which is mounted on the tank of a 1938 double-bar frame Autocycle, shows the clout that Schwinn must have had with its suppliers. Stimsonite produced it with the Schwinn script, which was certainly not an off-the-shelf item.

Left: Another outside supplier that Schwinn bought a lot of goods from was named Torrington. This company supplied handlebar stems and pedals like the deluxe model No.10 shown here. These were the highest-grade rubber pedals Schwinn could get and were used on the Autocycles.

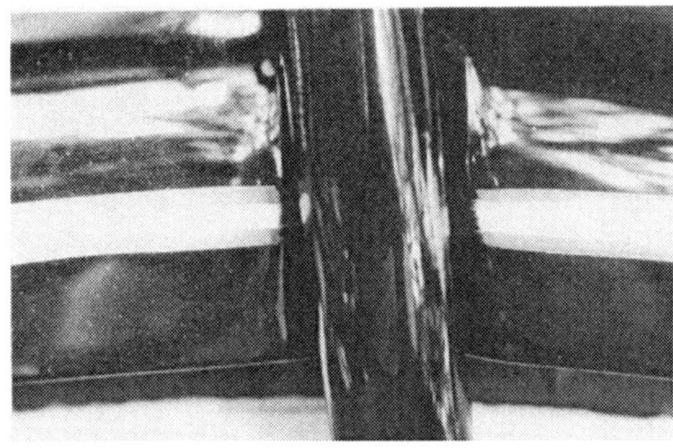

Ujszaszi duplicated the factory pinstriping used on the Autocycle, as shown here. In pinstriping the fender, the ends of the brushstrokes are visible where they stop for the frame dimple, just like Schwinn did it.

Below: The Black Phantom embodied all that Schwinn offered in balloon-tire bicycles at the time of its 1949 introduction. This 1950 example typifies the model that caught on with the kid market in a big way. This particular bike is original, except for the seat, pedals, rear reflector, and decals, which are all reproductions.

In keeping with the speedometer's image, the speedometer *drive* is an elaborate, heavy-duty mechanism as well.

concerted revival effort. Customers then were, and collectors now are, the benefactors of this exemplary effort.

Phantom

Somehow, Schwinn knew just how to tweak the B6 to appeal to the kids. Essentially, a new name, chrome fenders, and a new paint scheme were about all that was needed to create the classic Phantom bicycles. In 1949, kids all over the country had a new bike to add to their birthday or Christmas wish list: The Black Phantom. As Schwinn sales brochures described: "You've never seen such a bicycle! Completely equipped with every accessory imaginable to delight the eyes of every youngster. Finest Schwinn craftsmanship throughout. The proudest achievement of three generations of experience in designing and building fine bicycles makes the Phantom the most wonderful bicycle any boy can own!"

The equipment list *was* quite lengthy for the Phantom. It had chromed tubular rims,

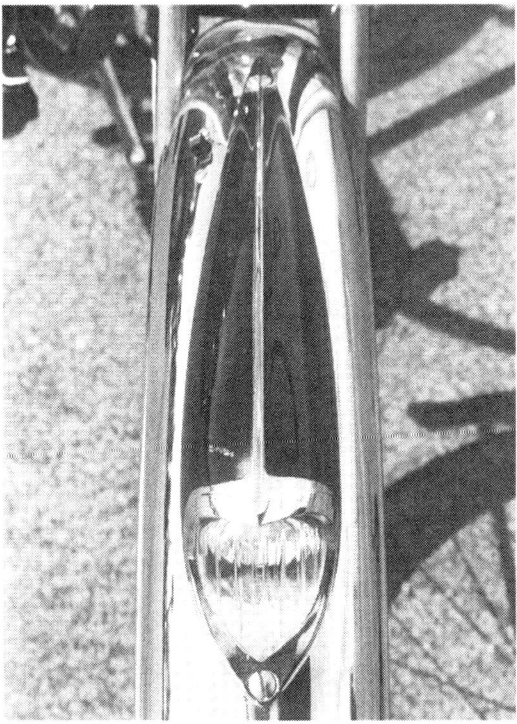

Schwinn believed that the streamlined front Fenderlite (introduced in 1940) was a good choice for the Phantoms. They were correct in that belief, as it is one of the defining classic features that helped re-popularize the Phantoms today.

The year 1946 was the first for the built-in Schwinn kickstand, and it was incorporated into the Phantom's features, as shown on this 1950 model.

Here are some more of the cool features that endeared the Phantoms to buyers 50 years ago and still do today: chromed and painted horn tank, Cycelock, and spring-fork suspension.

The 1949 Phantom chain guards were blank; by 1950, a stylish script logo was developed, as shown here.

chrome fenders, automatic stoplight, built-in kickstand, deluxe leather saddle, built-in horn, streamlined tank, extra length chain guard, built-in Cycelock, patented spring fork, Schwinn Fenderlite (a streamlined headlight), patented cantilever frame, and heavy-duty whitewall tires. The introductory model was called a Black Phantom, due to its paint scheme. It was finished predominantly in black, with red accents near the head tube, on the seat tube, and on the chain guard; the red accents were outlined with vivid white pinstriping. The Black Phantom name appeared on the chain guard in black script outlined in gold. The Black Phantom was truly a stunning beauty.

So, the look was right, the name was right, and the dealer network was poised to make the Black Phantom the object of desire for many youths throughout the next

Not every Phantom was black. Some were green, and others, like this 1950 Phantom, were red. The chain guard simply read "Phantom" on the green and red models.

decade. Initially, the Black Phantom was available only as a boys' 26-inch model. By the next year, 1950, a 24-inch juvenile model was offered, but it used a Delta Rocket Ray headlight instead of Schwinn's streamlined Fenderlite. Later the same year, two other Phantoms came to market; they had either red or green paint treatments, both with black accents. Their chain guards just read "Phantom." They were not called Red Phantoms or Green Phantoms, but were just Phantoms that happened to be red or green instead of black. The 24-inch Phantoms were only available through the 1954 model year, but in 1955 there was a girls' Phantom in the lineup that was blue. That experiment only lasted one year, and very few girls' Black Phantoms were built, so the girls' Phantoms are pretty hard to find now, but still less desirable than the boys' versions.

All of the Phantoms came with single-speed coaster brake rear hubs. The serial numbers for the early Phantoms (1949-1951) are stamped on the underside of the bottom bracket (crank hanger), and the numbers for the later Phantoms (1952-1959) appear on the frame near the left rear axle dropout. Phantom production ceased after 1959, as sportier, lighter middleweight models were catching on. At around 70 pounds, the Phantoms helped put the heavy in the term heavyweight, and that style was becoming outdated. The legacy of the Phantom had strong roots though, and this exciting model continues to be one of the most popular classic bicycles today. There was even a factory-sponsored reproduction Black Phantom built in 1995 to commemorate Schwinn's new owner, the Scott Sports Group, and Schwinn's centennial (1895-1995) celebration. The creation of those reproduction Black Phantoms validated the classic position that the original bikes hold.

Panther

For those who wished to spend less than the cost of a Phantom, the Schwinn Panther appeared in 1950. The Panthers were pretty well equipped, but they were built on the older Motorbike-type frame instead of the cantilever design. That old frame still had a good spot for the Panthers' horn tanks, along with the rest of the features. The Panthers all had the spring fork, Delta Rocket Ray headlight, chrome seat springs, chrome fenders, and a rear nine-hole rack. Colors available on the Panther were black and red, two-tone red, two-tone blue, or two-tone green. Many collectors prefer

The Panthers were introduced in 1950. They were lower priced than the Phantoms, but by no means economy models. They fell into the "equipped" category with extras like chrome fenders, spring forks, rear carriers, horn tanks, and headlights. As shown in this ad, they were offered in both boys' and girls' versions.

This unrestored green 1953 Panther is pretty complete for its age. It is missing the top half of its Delta Rocket Ray headlight, needs a whitewall up front, sports a vintage seat cover, and has dents and scrapes, but you won't see many unrestored examples in better condition.

The Panther tank seen here is fairly straight for its age (about 50 years). Also visible is the spring fork as it appeared on the Panther.

Panthers today strictly due to their appealing paint treatments.

The Panthers came out at a time when Schwinn was strengthening its dealer network and brand image. The number of total dealers was actually shrinking, but the ones that remained were well stocked total concept stores, in which sales and service personnel were well trained. Schwinn wanted buyers to be able to depend on getting competent product information and great service at any Schwinn dealer in the country. From 1950 to 1960, the number of authorized Schwinn dealers dropped from about 15,000 to 2,000. The quantity went down, but the quality went up. The Schwinn brand identification was increasing at this time. Schwinn enhanced this phenomenon by using the

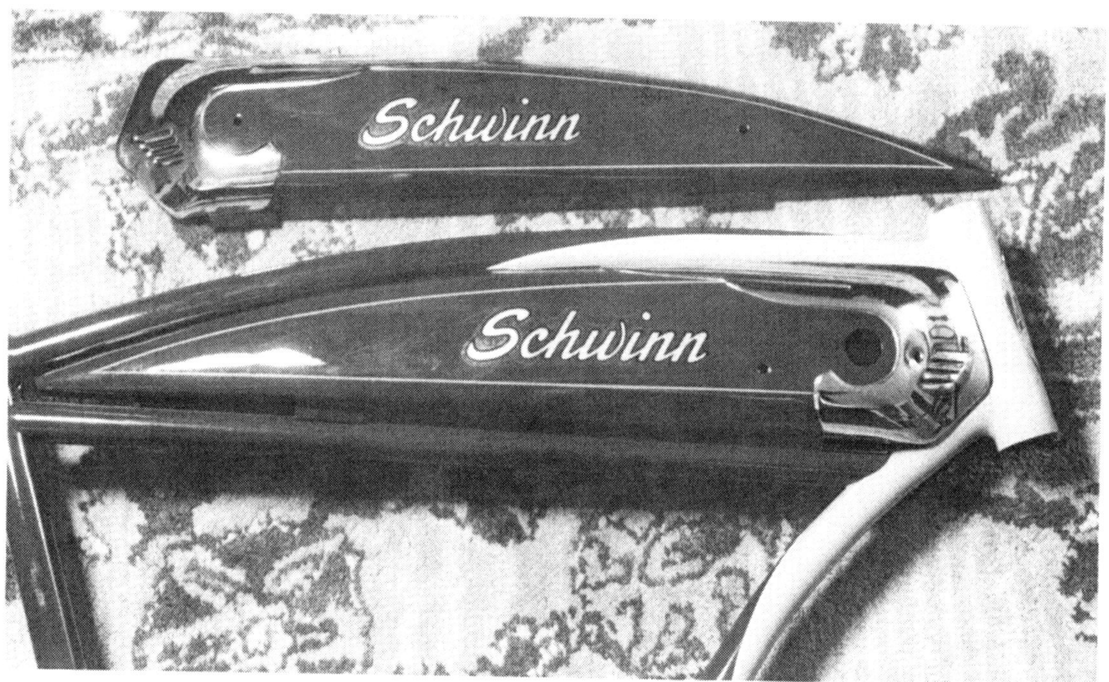

Dave Stromberger restored this Panther frame and tank to new condition. Don't try this at home, however, unless you're well practiced in body and paint work. Results of this quality take time, patience, and a lot of expertise.

Here's a Panther chain guard with its history (fading and scratches) showing.

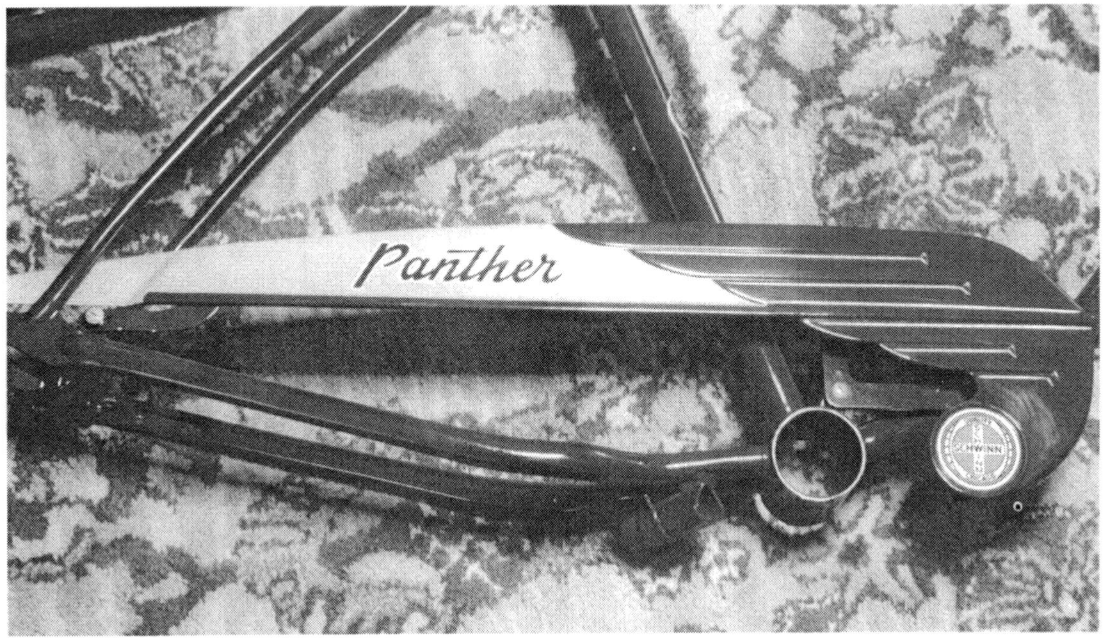

Here's a Panther chain guard after a master restorer like Stromberger has worked his magic on it; it included bodywork, paint, pinstripes, and decals.

Schwinn name more on its bikes. The Panther had its model name on the chain guard, but also had "Schwinn" script on the tank. Most of the head badges were now being made with the name Schwinn, instead of the many other names used in the past. By the mid-1950s, all Schwinns had Schwinn head badges.

The Panther model name was the first one with a feline reference, but others like Jaguar and Tiger would follow later. These names supplied a good product image, associating the bikes with the cat-like qualities of beauty, speed, and agility. The Panthers were sold in girls' as well as boys' versions. The heavyweight Panther only lasted through the 1954 model year, but later gained new life as a middleweight model.

Jaguar

On the subject of cats, one of the rarest Schwinn heavyweights was the feline-inspired Jaguar. This model got started in 1954, but only lasted through 1955, when the middleweights began taking over. The balloon-tire Jaguar had several qualities that made it unique in the marketplace.

The Jaguar was definitely classified as an equipped bicycle; it was missing several features, including a tank and a spring fork, but it had some one-of-a-kind characteristics. Schwinn, apparently influenced by import bikes, outfitted the balloon-tire Jag with some unlikely bedfellows: a British three-speed rear hub and hand-operated caliper brakes. This juxtaposition was heretofore unheard of. It created a wonderful character and mystique for the short-lived Jaguar, making this model an almost instant classic. The Jaguar came in black or red, and the red used a gold undercoat that gave the finish a special iridescence. Chrome fenders and rims were attached to a cantilever frame, riding on whitewall tires. A Delta Rocket Ray headlight painted to match

This 1954 balloon-tire Jaguar is both rare and unique. It is rare because it was only produced in 1954 and 1955. It is unique for many reasons, including the presence of a three-speed hub (no other heavyweights had it), hand brakes, and an interesting mix of accessories.

the bike set off this stylish assembly. There were no girls' or juvenile Jaguars produced.

The serial numbers for the heavyweight Jaguars are stamped at the left rear axle dropout, and should match up to the model years 1954 and 1955 (some may have 1953 frame numbers, but 1954 was the introductory model year). The timing was not quite right to continue production of the balloon-tire Jaguar, but the model name resurfaced on the Mark II middleweight Jaguar in 1957. The heavyweight Jaguars were not quite at the top of the model stratification, but they rank highly among classic, collectible Schwinns now.

Here is a close-up top view of the heavyweight Jaguar's Delta Rocket Ray front lamp.

One good thing about having a Sturmey-Archer three-speed hub is that the date of manufacture is stamped on the housing; the hub on this 1954 Jaguar is of the rare alloy type, as opposed to the more common chromed steel variety.

Right: Most of the original, deluxe-style seat tube decal still remains on this 1954 Jaguar.

Hollywood

While the equipped Schwinns like the Autocycles and Phantoms were satisfying the boys' market, the girls had some deluxe models of their own. The Hollywood was evidently supposed to play upon girls' aspirations to be stars. Schwinn used movie stars to advertise Hollywoods and other Schwinns as early as 1940. The Hollywood had great colors, lots of equipment, and was "Every bit as beautiful and graceful as the famous screen stars," according to Schwinn ads. The Hollywood was named in 1938, but the name only appeared in literature, not on the bike.

Equipment on the Hollywoods included the spring fork, expander brakes, whitewall tires, and a horn tank. The available colors were maroon, blue, and black. They all came with ivory trim, and Schwinn offered two-tone combinations as well. The pre-World War II models had lacing at the rear wheel to keep skirts out of the spokes; this lacing has disintegrated on most original bikes by now, but the multiple fender holes (to accommodate the lacing) are telltale signs of its early presence. Although the balloon-tire Hollywoods were only around until 1948 (when the new girls' Starlet models were introduced), the Hollywood name was resurrected for a middleweight model from 1957 until 1982.

This 1940 girls' Hollywood is original right down to the red natural rubber tires. Like other Hollywood bicycles of this era, this one sports plenty of equipment, including a spring fork, a horn tank, a streamlined Fenderlite, the big Stimsonite reflector, a chrome feather chain guard, and factory fender lacing (skirt guard). *Dave Stromberger*

Like the 1940 Autocycles, the horn button of this 1940 Hollywood was located on the tank (as opposed to the earlier handlebar location). Also notice the Excelsior badge, which was typical issue for that time period. *Dave Stromberger*

The owner of this 1951 Starlet added a front basket and handlebar streamers to suit her taste. As evident here, Schwinn also added a few goodies too, such as a horn tank, a rear carrier, fork truss rods, and a two-tone paint scheme of Summer Cloud White and Holiday Rose.

Starlet

In keeping with the show business theme, Schwinn introduced the Starlet in 1948. Schwinn's pitch to dealers proclaimed:

> All new for girls. Fashion styled colors. Only on Schwinn . . . "pedaling pastels." Special attractive pastel colors with great feminine appeal. The girls have all been waiting for them! Always first with the newest, Arnold, Schwinn & Co. offers the dealer the latest for girls' bicycles. Fashion design! Following the color trend of girls' fashion designers, Schwinn offers a new line of fashion style bicycles for the modern girls. Enthusiastically received by all who have seen them. Stock a complete line, they'll sell like hotcakes. Order these new perky pastels. Windswept Green and Luscious Lavender, or Summer Cloud White and Holiday Rose.

The Starlets were equipped models, sporting such accessories as horn tanks, rear racks, headlights and chrome rims. Optional equipment included the spring fork and whitewall tires. During this brand-conscious period, Schwinn placed a Starlet logo on the chain guard, and Schwinn script on the tank. Starlets are all coaster brake models, with serial numbers stamped under the bottom bracket. In the 1950s, Schwinn claimed that the Starlet was "dainty, luxurious, and completely feminine." That unique product philosophy gave this model some of its classic appeal today. Starlets came in 26-, 24-, and

20-inch models. Again, the girls' models don't create the same interest with collectors as equivalent boys' models, but some of the equipped girls' bikes, like the Starlet, rival some of the unequipped boys' bikes. Production of the heavyweight Starlet ended after the 1956 model year, and it was reissued as a middleweight in 1957.

Originally, the Starlet name appeared on this chain guard to the left of the partially visible star; unfortunately, after 50 years of use, decals tend to fade away.

As evident here, some of the lower-priced models like this 1941 DX still had style and equipment. The lesser models often used a skip-tooth sprocket (chain ring) and chain, where the sprocket teeth are spread wider than normal. This bike happens to have what is now called the sweetheart sprocket because of the heart shapes designed into it. And yes, those wild tank graphics are factory issue. *Bob Ujszaszi*

The DX models used a Delta three-rib Torpedo light on the front fender.

Other Heavyweights

There were many other balloon-tire (heavyweight) models turned out of the Schwinn factory before and after World War II. Most of these are unequipped variations of the aforementioned equipped models. Generally, the B series Schwinns are the cantilever-framed, equipped models, and the D or DX series are the older-style camelback-framed, lesser-equipped models. To confuse things, however, there are deluxe versions of the unequipped bikes, making them appear as fancy as the equipped models. As the practice of naming (as opposed to just numbering) the models gained momentum, the imaginations of Schwinn idea men got active. Someone must have had a fondness for insects, because the Hornet and the Wasp, or what one might call "bug bikes," debuted in the early 1950s.

This unequipped 1939 Excelsior Schwinn even has a spring fork and a Fore-wheel brake, so "unequipped" didn't mean absolutely plain.

This 1937 Excelsior Schwinn was labeled in the catalog as the "Girls' Popular Priced Model." This one is a bit more rare than usual because of its aluminum Gothic (as Schwinn called them) fenders. The unusual chain guard was a custom touch that was most likely dealer installed long ago.

This girls' D model is actually a Schwinn Meteor, although you have to dig through Schwinn promotional literature to figure that out, since there is no name identification on the bike. Even these basic balloon-tire bikes have classic style, with finishing touches like graphics and a front fender flare.

As naming of the models gained momentum, there were many to choose from. This Hornet had a logo unique to its model.

The Wasp logo had an angry look; this model actually represented the heavyweight line the longest, lasting through 1965.

Actually, the Hornet came out first, in 1951, and it even had a tank, rack, and headlight. With their painted fenders and rims, though, Hornets held a lower spot in the lineup than Phantoms and Panthers. The Hornets were built in boys', girls', and juvenile models. These are cool classics, because their lack of chrome makes them look even older than they are. The Hornet turned into a middleweight model in about 1956.

It was the Wasp that last carried the balloon-tire torch in its 1954 through 1964 tenure as a heavyweight model. The Phantom was phased out in 1959, so the Wasp was the lone heavyweight among middleweights and lightweights until 1965. Starting then, the closest thing to a balloon tire in the Schwinn line (until the Cruisers of the 1980s) was the rear tire on a Sting-Ray, or those on a Cycle Truck. The Wasp also came as a boys', girls', or juvenile bicycle, and was considered an unequipped, or standard model.

Even lower in cost than the Wasp was the popular priced Spitfire. That name has fairly timeless appeal; Spitfire was a good name for a bike 50 years ago, and it would sound well on a BMX bicycle today. There was no shortage of names tossed about at Schwinn, as evidenced by the steady flow of models. The Meteor, the Leader, and the Streamliner were also model names used on Schwinn heavyweights. These bikes were all offered as boys', girls', and juvenile bikes except the Streamliner, which was basically a renamed B6 (Autocycle) model.

It is hard to go wrong by saving any balloon-tire Schwinn. Sure, there are variants in desirability, condition, and value, but the essential classic ingredients are present in all of them. They have sustained their following through a test-of-time period, and show no signs of losing that appeal. Schwinn used to say that you would "Smile at the miles" when you rode a Schwinn. That still holds true today, except they also make us smile when they're sitting still.

Chapter 4

Classic Middleweight Schwinns

★★★½	Corvette (boys')
★★½	Corvette (girls')
★★★½	Jaguar
★★★	American (boys')
★★	American (girls')
★★★	Tiger (boys')
★★	Tiger (girls')
★★★	Panther
★★★	Deluxe Typhoon
★★½	Typhoon
★★	Tornado
★★	Hollywood
★★★	Debutante
★★★	Fair Lady
★★	Co-Ed
★★½	Starlet (II & III)
★★½	Other boys' middleweights
★★	Other girls' middleweights

By the 1950s, Schwinn bicycles had the durability image mastered for sure, but the ever-present lighter import bikes had a sporty appeal that wooed some buyers. Many people now saw the balloon-tire heavyweights— with their tanks, racks, and other accessories—as clumsy and outdated. Too bad we couldn't have bought a few Phantoms at fire-sale prices when this attitude prevailed. The lightweight model bicycles from Schwinn never really competed effectively against the imports in the 1950s, due to the higher cost and excess weight of the Schwinns. Rather than compete head-

Girls' Corvettes were available right from the start, like the 1957 model shown here. The sport pedals, crash bar seat, and the front rack are standard equipment; the owner added the high-rise handlebars in 1965. The girls' Corvettes were discontinued in 1959, as other new deluxe girls' models came out.

on, Schwinn developed a bike that was still just as durable and stylish as the existing heavyweights, but lighter. This new bicycle was marketed as a sporty American bike that would outlast the lighter import. These so-called middleweights came to market in 1954 and were the bicycles of choice for many millions of riders through the 1950s and 1960s.

Within two years following the middleweight debut, several models were added to the lineup, and middleweight sales led all other Schwinn lines. The reason that these models were ready for market so quickly is that research had begun on such products as early as 1952. This research was a necessary response to the importing of European lightweight bicycles, which were generally lighter and cheaper. This same market response would be the basis for Schwinn's future use of multi-speed derailleurs and the production of lighter bikes like the Varsity. But at this time (1955–1969), Schwinn hit the nail on the head with the middleweight models when it came to a bike that got top marks for durability, ride, and style. Even as lightweights and Sting-Rays were dominating the Schwinn lineup, the middleweight Typhoon and Hollywood bicycles were offered all the way through 1982.

The announcement of the new middleweight lineup in 1954 proceeded with much fanfare and success. There was a lot of anticipation and excitement created over what really amounted to the use of a narrower tire. The new width for the middleweight tires was 1-3/4 inches, as opposed to the 2.125-inch heavyweight tires; the new rim designation was S-7, instead of the earlier S-2 heavyweight rim.

Actually, the middleweight models didn't weigh much less than the ballooners, and the middleweights remaining today are often erroneously identified as heavyweights. For sure, heavyweight lineage was the basis for the middleweight styling. For boys' bikes, the middleweight frame was a copy of the by-then-famous heavyweight cantilever frame that had been used on earlier models, including the Autocycle, Phantom, and Panther. The middleweight lineup also included juvenile (20-inch tires), youth (24-inch tires), and girls' (step-through frame) versions.

The biggest change for the premier of the middleweight line was the new, narrower rim (1-3/4 inch), dubbed the S-7. It had the same tubular design as the balloon-tire S-2 rim, but took a 1-3/4 inch-wide tire, instead of the 2.125 inch-wide, low-pressure balloon tire. The new tire held pressure in the 45-50 pounds-per-square-inch range, so there was less rolling resistance than with the balloon tires that held less air pressure. These tires, along with lighter parts and fewer accessories, made these new models sportier than their heavier predecessors. With less rolling resistance from the tires, and the addition of two-speed and three-speed hubs, the bikes were easier to pedal; a special Corvette model even had a five-speed derailleur in 1961 and 1962.

Schwinn's dealer literature described these bicycles as "light balloon" (a designation that did not seem to stick), but the bikes still weighed about 50 pounds. The staple of the classic middleweight design was the cantilever frame, which was used on the majority

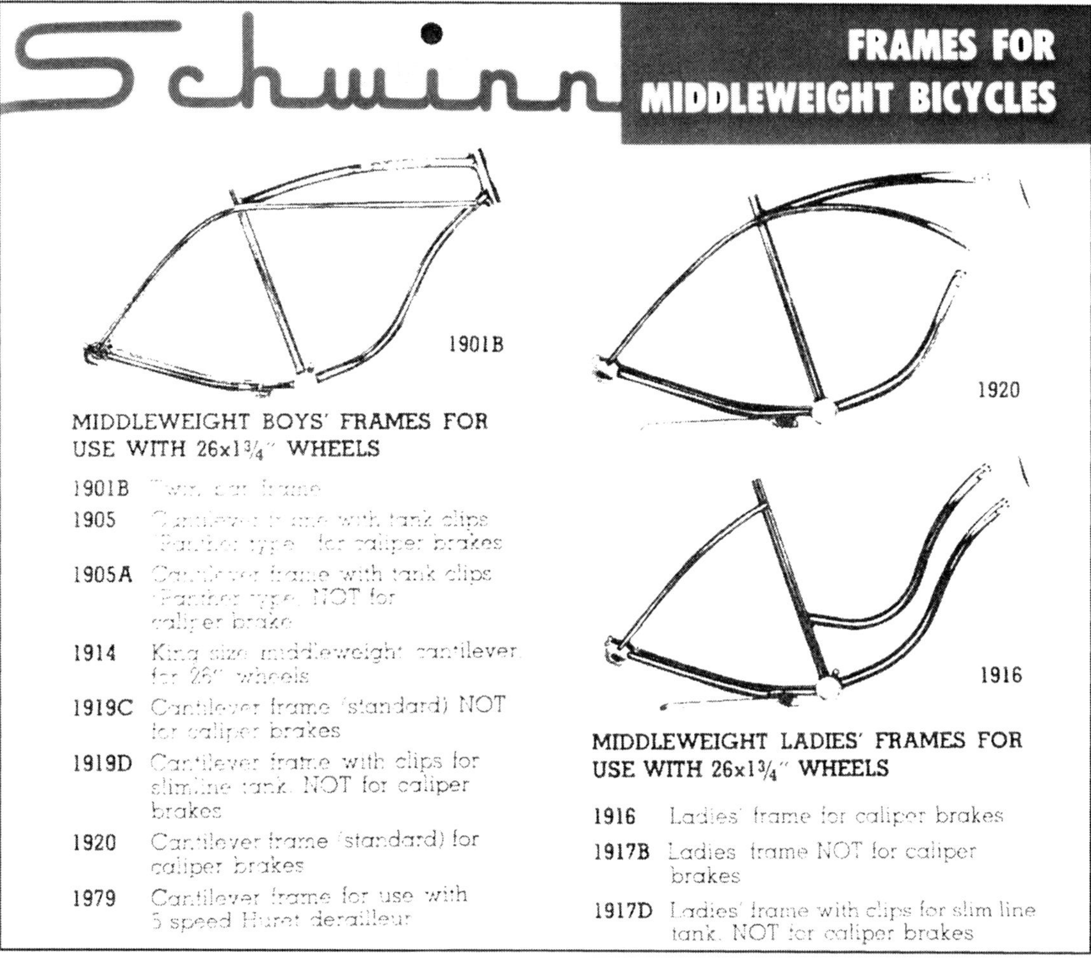

Schwinn FRAMES FOR MIDDLEWEIGHT BICYCLES

1901B

1920

1916

MIDDLEWEIGHT BOYS' FRAMES FOR USE WITH 26x1¾" WHEELS

1901B Twin bar frame

1905 Cantilever frame with tank clips (Panther type) for caliper brakes

1905A Cantilever frame with tank clips (Panther type) NOT for caliper brake

1914 King size middleweight cantilever for 26" wheels

1919C Cantilever frame (standard) NOT for caliper brakes

1919D Cantilever frame with clips for slimline tank. NOT for caliper brakes

1920 Cantilever frame (standard) for caliper brakes

1979 Cantilever frame for use with 5 speed Huret derailleur

MIDDLEWEIGHT LADIES' FRAMES FOR USE WITH 26x1¾" WHEELS

1916 Ladies' frame for caliper brakes

1917B Ladies frame NOT for caliper brakes

1917D Ladies' frame with clips for slim line tank. NOT for caliper brakes

Since its introduction in 1938, the cantilever frame was the foundation for most Schwinn heavyweight bicycles; it would be the same for the middleweights. The majority of boys' models used a frame like number 1920 shown here; an exception was the straight bar cantilever frame number 1901B, which was used on the introductory Typhoon (1962 only), and a few other models such as the Flying Star. The girls' bikes all had the step-through version, like number 1916.

of boys' models, with a few exceptions. During the Typhoon's first year (1962), the Tornado and the Flying Star used a slightly modified cantilever that had straight rather than curved lower bars, from the head tube to the seat down tube. As with the boys' bikes, the girls' middleweights borrowed their frame design from the heavyweights. Some of the middleweight models are boys' only, and some are girls' only, while other models were built in both versions. Now we will explore some particular features of the various classic middleweights.

Corvette

How do you create a sporty image for a new line of bicycles? You might name the introductory model after America's new sports car: the 1953 Corvette. That is exactly what the Schwinn marketing group did with their first middleweight. For buyers wanting speed, or at least the image of speed, the 1954 Corvette bicycle led the start of a line of bikes. The Corvette automobile was also marketed with a speed image, and since Schwinn showed a history of associating the images of their bicycles with cars and motorcycles, naming the Corvette bicycle was a natural process. The only surprising situation is that Schwinn was able to use the name without infringing on trademark rights. Nevertheless, Schwinn marketed the Corvette as a top-of-the-line middleweight from 1954 through 1965. (It was called the Corvette II for its final year.)

The Corvette was like a fresh slate; the name was not a carryover from the heavyweights, as with some other models, so there was no tired image to shed. Beginning with its introduction, the Corvette model was a leader in standard and optional equipment. It was by no definition an economy model. Back in the 1950s and 1960s, the Schwinn Corvette had all of the ingredients of a future classic, which it certainly is now. Schwinn was also a leader in marketing to females; the Corvette, a bike that might have been considered kind of macho, was available in girls' versions right from the start. The ladies' Corvette was discontinued in 1959, however, when more girl-exclusive models like the Fair Lady and Debutante were added to the Schwinn line.

With its unveiling and production in 1954, the Corvette was recognized as Schwinn's first middleweight, but it wasn't actually available to the public for the first time until the 1955 model lineup. Nonetheless, there are undoubtedly some old Corvettes around with 1954 serial numbers on their frames, since the year of frame production does not always dictate the model year. The serial numbers are located at the left rear axle dropout on the frame for all of the Corvette series, and these numbers can all be referenced for approximate year-of-production dating. All of the boys' Corvettes were based on the then- (and now-) famous cantilever frame design; the girls' Corvettes used the step-through frame.

There were initially two Corvette model choices available besides the boys' or girls' designations. The 1955 Corvette was offered with either a cable-operated three-speed hub or a single-speed coaster brake; both versions were deluxe models with whitewall tires and a front carrier. The carrier, or front rack, on these early Corvettes was a classic in its own right. The rack was a German-made double-hinged aluminum alloy contraption designed to hold books or a lunchbox securely,

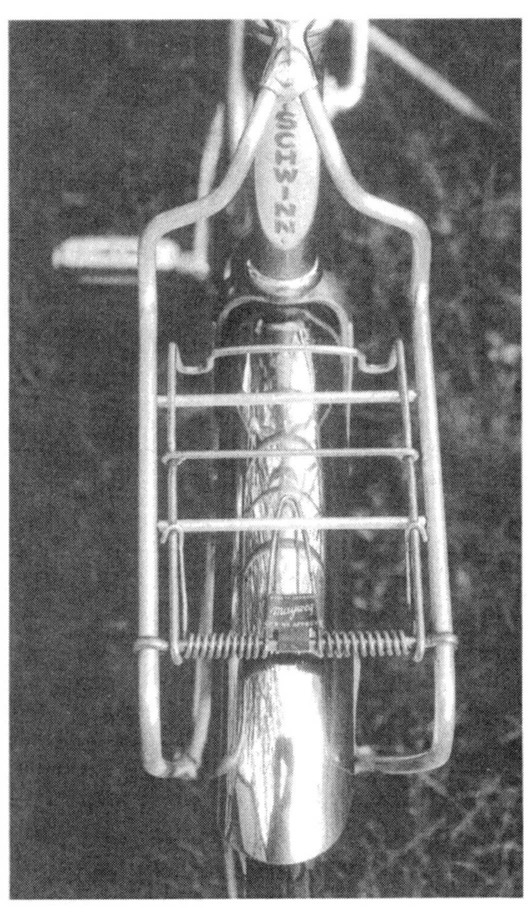

The Corvette front rack was a "Schwinn Approved" product that was imported from the German Mayweg Company.

with the hinged portion of the rack remaining parallel to its base. This foreign-manufactured, "Schwinn Approved" carrier was typical of the bicycle industry's ahead-of-its-time approach to manufacturing and assembly, where international cooperation was evident. Most of the imported components used on these bikes were labeled "Schwinn Approved," exemplifying the clout that Schwinn had with manufacturers. This influence was undoubtedly due to the large volume of parts Schwinn was buying from these various foreign suppliers.

The three-speed models used European cable-operated rear hubs and caliper-style hand-operated brakes. Corvettes with this option required an extra bracket on the frame to accommodate the rear brake, and a front fork casting with a built-in hole for the front brake. The frames and forks with these provisions were also used on most coaster brake Corvettes; other middleweights, such as the Typhoon, didn't have a place for caliper brakes if the bike came with coaster brakes. The gear selector lever was mounted on the right-hand side of the handlebars.

In addition to the preceding choices, you could buy a 24-inch Corvette through the model-year 1961. The smaller model was probably sold in very low numbers, so it would be a relatively rare model to find today. Over the years of the Corvette model run, the Schwinn factory offered the colors of black, red ("Flamboyant"), blue, green, and gold ("Coppertone"). Judging by what is remaining today, the biggest-selling Corvette models

This was the seat tube decal used on Corvettes through 1958.

In 1959 and after, this new, more ornate seat tube decal appeared on the Corvette models.

This 1961 Corvette is a single-speed, coaster brake model with the classic cantilever frame. Also shown here is the newer chromed and painted chain guard introduced in 1959, sport pedals (now often called "bow" pedals), and a chrome fork crown. Two other classic touches are the teardrop-shaped rear reflector and the double-hinged lunchbox carrier. (See more photos in next section: Jaguar).

were boys' 26-inch versions, with three-speed hubs, in the color of black or red. But there are still plenty of other Corvette variations around to satisfy just about every taste.

Another option made available right in the middle of the Corvette production run was the Bendix Automatic two-speed rear coaster brake hub. This is the sought-after hub for which you use a kick-back, or slight back-pedal, motion to change gears. Often called the triple-band hub because of its three yellow or red painted stripes on the outer

Due to apparent influence from imported bikes, Schwinn introduced the unusual Corvette depicted in this ad mat in 1961: A five-speed derailleur model! This was an obscure match-up that was only produced for two years; both its oddity and rarity add greatly to its classic status today.

shell, this hub was well received when it was introduced in 1960. Through the following decade, Schwinn sold a lot of middleweight bicycles equipped with the Bendix Automatic (sometimes called multi-speed) hub. The automatic function was the downshift that took place when you began to stop after pedaling along in high gear. With the rearward rotation required to activate the coaster brake, the hub automatically shifted to low gear for your next takeoff; after you got going, you had to make the slightly less automatic shift back to high gear by back-pedaling just enough to shift without applying the brake.

Speaking of gears, a new multi-speed Corvette hit the market in 1961: a five-speed derailleur model! This one was only available in the boys' 26-inch versions, and the target market was not certain. Americans, especially children, were not familiar with derailleur shifters, and changing gears was difficult for them. This five-speed setup probably was not suited for most of the middleweight riders, so this Corvette was discontinued after only two model years. The quirkiness of the five-speed Corvette is exactly what causes its classic appeal today; unfortunately, its remaining examples are relatively few, due to its original lack of popularity and limited model run. Schwinn advertising copy touted, "the most thrilling ride ever!" along with, "Fast starts . . . effortless hill climbs . . . and jet fast straightaways." Those promises didn't reel in enough buyers back then, but now the 1961 and 1962 Schwinn five-speed

The seat tube decal for the derailleur-equipped Corvette is obviously exclusive to that model alone.

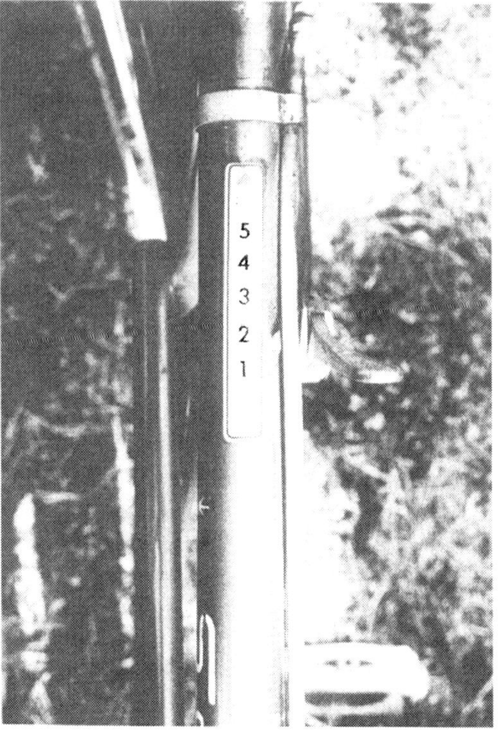

Schwinn mounted the shifter for the five-speed Corvette on the top bar, and applied a decal to denote gear positions.

It's very unusual to see a derailleur on a middleweight Schwinn bicycle. That is because the 1961 and 1962 Corvettes are the only Schwinns to have them.

Corvettes must be placed near the top of any most desirable middleweight list.

The entire Corvette lineup was defined in Schwinn's vernacular as bicycles that were equipped, as opposed to un-equipped. They could also be described as loaded versus plain. The presence of multiple speeds, headlights, whitewall tires, hand brakes, racks, and extra chrome are all qualities of a classic bicycle. Even the graphic decal on the Corvette seat down tube is very ornate, and signifies the equipped model. The more deluxe the model, however, the more things there are to be broken or missing. If you are evaluating an old Corvette, be aware of missing items like carriers or a faulty three-speed hub. These are likely faults of old machines, but value adjustments must be made for missing accessories or necessary mechanical repairs.

Corvettes have got to be placed near the top of the classic Schwinn list; they have all the right classic ingredients to make them great looking, interesting vintage bicycles. Since they were not introduced until 1954, they will need some more time to get near the top of the value list, but their value is headed one way: up!

Jaguar

Whereas many of the new middleweight models sported fresh, middleweight-exclusive names, the Jaguar initially existed as a heavyweight. The older balloon-tire heavyweight Jaguar was discontinued in 1955, and after a one-year hiatus, a middleweight version appeared in 1957: the Jaguar Mark II. Through its various versions and until its discontinuation in 1966, the Jaguar (a.k.a. the Mark II, Mark IV, Mark V, and Mark VI) was touted in Schwinn sales literature as "the finest fully equipped middleweight in the Schwinn Line."

What's in a name? In the case of the Schwinn Jaguar, it is at least a reference to the British automobile bearing the same name. This time, Schwinn chose a name with a dual association: one reference to a sport and luxury auto, and one to a fast and ferocious feline. It is again surprising that, as with the Corvette, Schwinn freely used the Jaguar name at the same time as the automaker, without being accused of trademark infringement. Even the Mark series was in use by the Lincoln automobile concurrent with Schwinn's use of that designation. In those simpler times, it was evidently considered acceptable.

None of the Schwinn Jaguars were ever offered in girls' models; all of them were equipped with the ever-popular cantilever frame. The introductory middleweight Jaguar, the Mark II, was produced in 1957 and 1958. All of the Jaguars are equipped bicycles, and the Mark II's equipment list included a Phantom-style tank with horn, front and rear carriers, front and rear lights, whitewall tires, caliper brakes, and a deluxe seat. The Mark IV (there was no Mark III) had a four-year production run from 1959 through 1962. The Mark IV was a deluxe bike, of course, with only a few changes from the Mark II. A new chrome rear rack,

For 1957 and 1958, the Jaguars carried the Mark II designation. As this 1958 model exemplifies, these were well-equipped bicycles. This one is almost all original, but it is missing its Phantom-style taillight, and the owner has added mud flaps.

For the years 1959 through 1962, the Jaguars were all Mark IV models. The 1960 model shown here is very original, but the Phantom-style horn tank is missing, along with the headlight. Notice the new chromed and painted chain guard that was used on the Mark IV bikes, as well as the new rear rack.

This teardrop-shaped rear reflector was used on the Mark IV Jaguars, as well as on other deluxe middleweight models like Corvette and Fair Lady. The plastic housing on this reflector was initially chromed, but very few of these have much chrome left today. The plating was very thin, and quickly wore down to the white plastic beneath.

The Mark IV models proudly display the ornate, deluxe decal on their seat tubes.

with four reflectors, replaced the painted four-hole Phantom-style rack that was present on the Mark II. A more modern finned chain guard superseded the old hockey-stick shape, and a stylish new teardrop-shaped reflector adorned the rear fender.

The most significant changes of the 1963 Jaguar Mark V were the replacement of the Phantom-style tank with a new slim-line design, and the addition of the earlier-style spring fork front suspension. Mark V production lasted through 1964, and the final Jaguar, the Mark VI, debuted in 1965. There were no notable changes with the new Mark

The double-hinged Jaguar carrier is designed to carry a lunchbox, books, or other large loads quite securely.

The serial numbers for the Jaguars, and all other middleweights before 1970, are stamped on the frame just above the left rear axle nut. Also notice (from the back side) how the chain guard starts out all-chrome; the front side is partially painted for the paint and chrome look.

This 1962 ad mat shows that the Mark IV models were equipped with the Phantom-style tanks and large headlights.

VI other than the name, and the fact that it could no longer be had with a three-speed rear hub (only one- and two-speed hubs with coaster brakes were offered). Over the entire Jaguar production, hub options and color availability varied, but one-, two-, and three-speeds, and red, black, and gold were all represented at some point. The serial number location for all of the Schwinn Jaguars is at the left rear axle dropout on the frame, and can be referenced to determine the years of production.

There is probably no particular standout year for the Jaguar series. The Mark V and the Mark VI are the most rare, because fewer of them were produced as popularity waned. This doesn't necessarily make them more sought after today, however, because the earlier Mark II and Mark IV possess the more old fashioned parts and pieces, such as the Phantom-style tank. The Mark V is unique because it is the only one that came with a spring-type front fork. So it's easy to see that there are many subtle characteristics that may reach out and grab you. As always, personal tastes determine preferences in collecting. Condition being equal, all of the middleweight Jaguars share generally equal demand at this time.

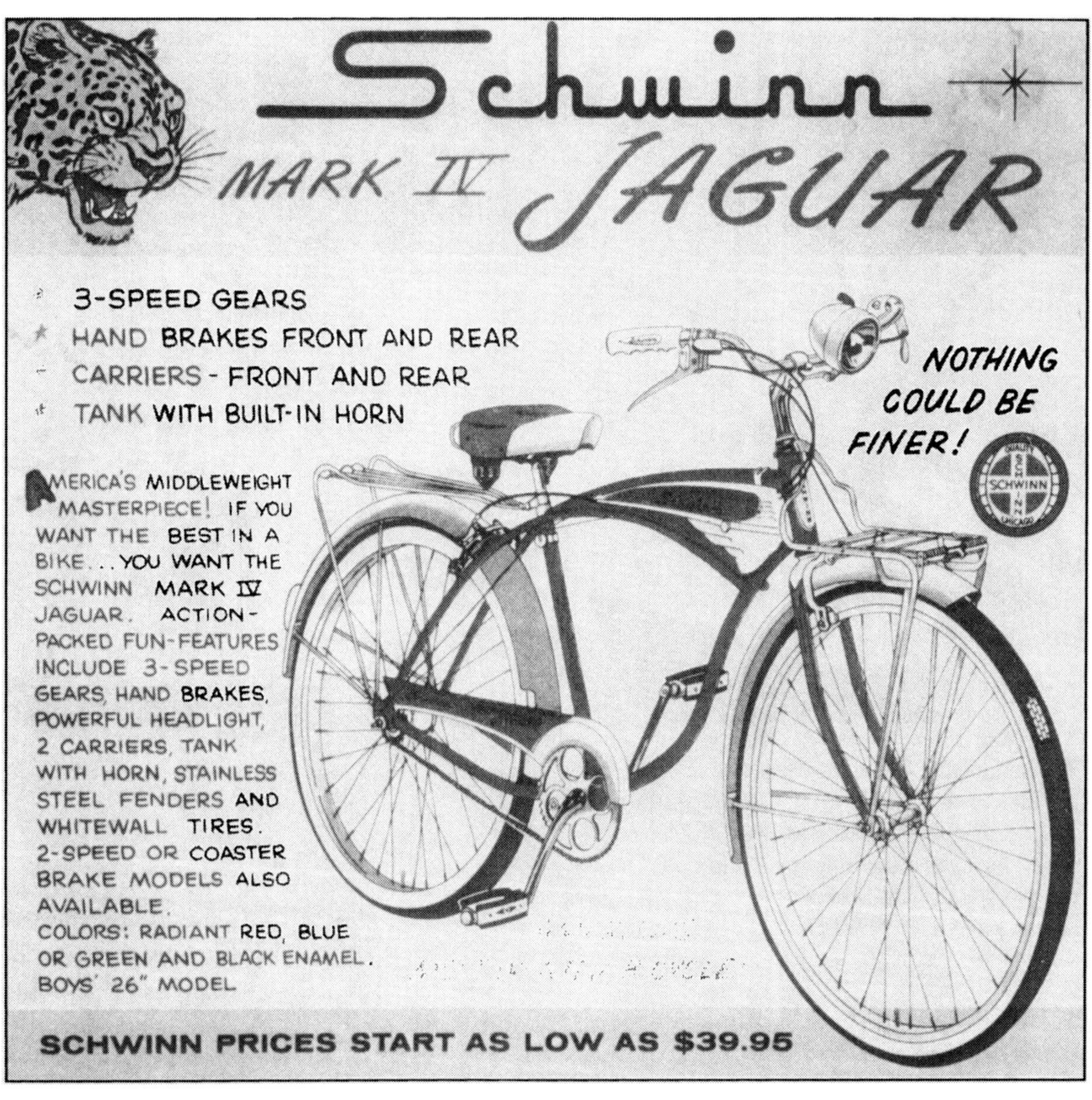

The copy on the back page of this 1959 Schwinn comic book represents the way the company made its appeal to kids.

As previously noted, the Schwinn Jaguar was not offered with a girls' frame, and it was never offered in the 20-inch or 24-inch juvenile sizes either. Sometimes, hobbyists will piece together their own versions of such things, but be assured that the Jaguars from the Schwinn factory were all 26-inch, boys'-frame bicycles. The Jaguar line was of the equipped, loaded, or premium type, and in addition to all of their standard features, each Jaguar had the ornate decal on the seat down tube.

Like other premium models, the Jaguars have many accessories that may become lost or broken over the years. Be sure to give proper credit to bikes you find that are complete, and deduct accordingly for missing or damaged items. Even an incomplete Jaguar

The Mark V and Mark VI Jaguars made use of this new slimline horn tank.

is a worthwhile treasure, because you can eventually find most of the missing parts to make it complete, or use the parts to make another one complete. Because of their position at the top of the middleweight lineup and their abundance of equipment, Schwinn Jaguars are significant classics to seek, find, obtain, and behold.

American

The influx of European bikes into the American market influenced the formation of the middleweights, and also had an effect on the model lineup. The increased awareness of imports caused many American customers to favor domestic products for patriotic reasons. Schwinn smartly capitalized on this pro-American sentiment by introducing the aptly named Schwinn American series. The impetus for this model name was to promote the fact that this bicycle was 100 percent American made. Advertising from the period touted, "every part quality built in the U.S.A." The name of the new middleweight was a departure from the more typical auto, animal, or insect references, but it was a good idea, since the American model proved to be a sales success.

Like the Corvette and Tiger, the American first showed up at dealer showrooms as a 1955 model, the first year for middleweights. The American was available in both boys' and girls' models, and both 24- and 26-inch versions right from the start. The boys' bikes all employed the tried-and-true cantilever frame, and the girls' bikes had the familiar step-through, low-bar frame. The distinction

The main pitch for the Schwinn Americans was proudly displayed on the fender of this bicycle. Schwinn and their dealers did their best to stir up anti-import sentiment at the time.

This 1964 Deluxe American carries some desirable equipment, such as a slimline tank, a front carrier, bow pedals, and whitewall tires. The generator-powered headlight was dealer installed.

In the mid-1960s, Schwinn did some reverse screening on certain chain guards, as shown on this 1964 model.

that one of the American models had, however, was being the first 20-inch middleweight offered. The 1955 dealer price sheet shows availability of both boys' and girls' 20-inch coaster brake American models. By 1956, the 20-inch girls' editions were discontinued, once again showing how quickly things can come and go in a relatively small factory controlled by one family.

The American production continued through 1958, but disappeared from the catalog in 1959. This was only a production respite though, since the American models were back in the lineup for the 1961 model year, until their final discontinuation in 1966. There are probably some 1961 Americans in existence with 1960 serial numbers, but officially there were no 1959 or 1960 models produced. The serial numbers for all of the Americans are stamped on the frame at the left rear axle dropout, and are traceable.

American models were built for both boys and girls. This 1964 girls' American has been outfitted with whitewall tires, a generator-powered taillight, and a Schwinn accessory rack from the same period.

The 1961 American was only available with the newly introduced Bendix Automatic two-speed hub for the 24- and 26-inch models. There was also a 20-inch American in 1961, which was only offered with a single-speed coaster brake hub. In 1962, the American lineage expanded in some interesting directions. In addition to the standard model, three new varieties of Americans were offered: The Deluxe American, the King Size American, and the Heavy Duty American. Making the deluxe bicycle was a typical undertaking, and included extras such as a slimline tank (with horn), a fender-mounted headlight, chrome rear carrier, and whitewall tires. The other two new models were not so typical. According to Schwinn literature, the King Size American was for tall teenagers and adults, and had an extra-large cantilever frame with a longer dimension of the seat down tube and of the head tube (between the fork and the handlebars). The King Size American was the only middleweight offered this way, and was available in 1962, 1963, and 1964. The Heavy Duty American was in the catalog those same three years, and was unique because of its heavy-duty spokes (120 gauge), along with a heavy-duty front hub and seat.

In 1965, Schwinn had one more trick up its sleeve for the American. That was the only year they offered an American with a front spring-type fork. The standard American was still in the lineup, but the Deluxe, the King Size, and the Heavy Duty were gone. In the catalog and price listings, the spring-fork model was simply dubbed, "American w/Spring-fork." All things considered, the Americans were not high-end or low-end in the middleweight lineup, but rather somewhere in the middle.

The seat tube decals for the American models displayed a patriotic stars and stripes shield. The words "Made in U.S.A." are now mostly faded, but originally appeared right above the shield. At the top is the ever-present "Quality Seal."

Over the years that the Americans were sold, all of the colors were represented: blue, red, green, gold, and black. The Americans had some markings that were exclusive to them, including a red, white and blue crest that appeared on the seat down tube and on the chain guard. Some even had a sticker on the rear fender proclaiming, "100 percent American Made." Advertising for the Americans stated, "If you demand a fine quality American-made product . . . beautifully finished and impressively designed . . . the Schwinn American is your choice." That statement holds up even today.

In general, all American models are more than worthy of their classic status, but there were some special models that stand out. Any 20-inch American qualifies, and certainly the King Size, Heavy Duty, and spring-fork models must be considered among the most desirable middleweight Schwinns. All of the American models were marketed specifically to coincide with a buy-American sentiment, which gave them one more unique classic characteristic. Sadly, it was difficult then for an all-American product to compete price-wise in the market, and it is even more difficult to do so today. Both then and now, parts are seldom built better, but they are often built cheaper in foreign countries. Without tariffs on imports, American products cost more because of our high standard of living. The Schwinn American bicycle exemplifies this slice of economic history; an all-American product must be marketed on virtues other than price, such as quality and patriotism. Despite these economic realities, don't pass up one of these historic classics if you find one.

The Schwinn Tigers were near the middle of the middleweight lineup in regard to price and equipment. The chrome fenders, sport pedals, front rack, and whitewall tires were all original equipment on this 1961 model. As usual, that cantilever frame is at the core of its classic look.

Tiger

The only animal in the initial middleweight group was the "big cat" model, the Tiger, which lived in the Schwinn lineup from 1955 through 1964. The Tiger designation was a new model name coined with the advent of the middleweights, and not a carryover from the balloon models. The marketing position for the Tiger was about in the middle of the equipped-to-unequipped range, making it a semi-deluxe model. Wherever it ranked then, the Tiger warrants respectable classic status today.

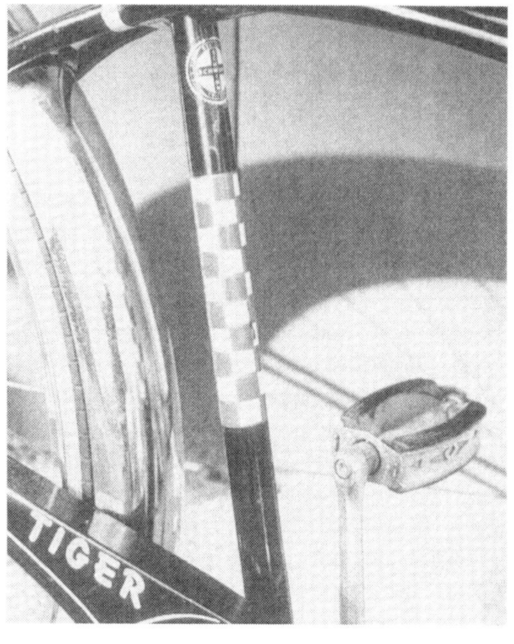

The Tigers got a special checkered seat tube decal, along with the Schwinn "Quality Seal" decal. Also shown here is the kind of clear, crisp chain guard lettering you are lucky to find today on bikes over 40 years old.

This picture shows at least two important facts: Parts from older bikes fit newer bikes, and owners like to customize. The owner of this 1961 Tiger has installed an early (1949 design) Phantom-style horn tank and a headlight; the rack is standard.

The first-year Tiger (1955) did not come standard with many accessories, and initially it was only available with the three-speed hub and hand-operated caliper brakes. This made it a fairly standard bike, with the not-so-standard inclusion of the hub and brake setup. For the first two years, you could purchase a Tiger as a boys' or girls' model, and you could choose either a 26-inch adult or 24-inch juvenile version. By 1957, the 24-inch choice disappeared, and in 1959 the girls' Tigers were pulled from the lineup. Schwinn was not giving up on the girls, but rather they were introducing new girls-exclusive models at this time.

Schwinn also began offering one-, two-, and three-speed Tigers in 1959 to give the bike a wider market appeal. The three-speed hubs did not hold up as well as the coaster brake hubs under severe use, which was the type of use many boys had in mind for their bicycles. Without apparent reason, the 24-inch models came back for sale in 1959, staying in the lineup with the 26-inch model through 1962, when the juvenile Tiger was discontinued for good. The 26-inch boys' versions in green, red, blue, or black represented the Tiger line for its final two years of production: 1963 and 1964. Because of their years of production, all of the Tigers' serial numbers appear on the frame at the left rear axle dropout and are traceable.

It is apparent that there is some redundancy among the various Schwinn models in regard to style and equipment. If you look closely, however, there is usually some feature unique to any given model. For the Tiger models, one of those features is the decal on the seat tube. A checkered design was chosen for application to the Tiger, lending it a sporty, as opposed to deluxe, image. Schwinn advertising touted, "The lightning-fast Schwinn Tiger is the bike to buy if you're looking for easy middleweight handling plus outstanding Schwinn style features."

Tiger is a classic name for a classic bicycle. The word *Tiger* has helped create an exciting image for products ranging from a sports car to gasoline, and even breakfast cereal (Tony the Tiger). Why not use it for a bicycle? Schwinn did, and created a lot of cool "cats" in the process.

The two-speed Bendix Automatic rear hubs were a Tiger option, and were identified by the three stripes on the housing, along with lettering on the brake arm, as shown.

Panther

Speaking of cats, there was yet another one that sounded good to Schwinn for a bicycle name: Panther. For those who didn't identify with the Jaguar or Tiger, Schwinn resurrected the Panther name from an old balloon-tire model, introducing the new Panther II in 1959. Maybe three cats were too many, however, since after the new model became a Panther III in 1960, it was discontinued in 1962. There was a reissue of the Panther for the 1966–1970 model years, but the Roman numeral designations were dropped. It was still a deluxe bicycle, but the ornate decal on the seat down tube was replaced with the circular Schwinn "criss-cross" decal. Their relatively short model run, of course, places the Panther II and Panther III among the most desirable middleweights today.

The Panthers were identified as deluxe or equipped models. Beginning with its middleweight introduction in 1959, the Panther II had the full host of features as standard equipment. The goody list included

This tank was used for the 1959 Panther II and the 1960 Panther III. It was a first-time design, and only used for this period, making it very rare.

When the next-generation Panthers came to market (1966–1970), they had the new slimline tank shown here.

The later Panthers (1966–1970) had a simple painted chain guard with this silk-screened logo.

a new trim-style horn tank, twin headlights, front and rear carriers, and whitewall tires. Schwinn advertising claimed that the "new style and new features" caused the Panther II to be "Fast! Sleek!" and "Powerful!" That last characteristic seems to be more dependent on the rider rather than the bike, but it made for good ad copy at the time.

According to Schwinn's marketing department, "The new Schwinn Panther is as sleek as a jungle cat! This great new bike will spring into action at the touch of your toe. . . ." It's obvious that associations and images were an important part of the model names, and Schwinn advertising attempted to capitalize on them. Schwinn offered the Panthers with one-, two-, or three-speed hubs, so the buyers could choose their own level of power.

As with the Jaguar, the Panthers only came in 26-inch boys' models both in the II and III series. The colors offered were black,

Schwinn had more than one version of chromed rear carriers. The proper one for this 1967 Panther is shown.

red, blue, and green. Being deluxe bikes, the Panthers had the ornate seat down tube decal (except from 1966 to 1970) and the teardrop-shaped rear reflector. The serial numbers for all of the Panther middleweights are stamped on the frame near the left rear axle dropout.

Panthers II and III are terrific classic finds today; their limited run along with their style and equipment assure this. It might be hard to find one; harder still is finding one with all of its equipment such as tanks, headlights, and racks intact. Good luck in your search!

Typhoon

By 1962, Arnold, Schwinn & Company had marketed many successful nameplates through its lines of bicycles. Animals (Panther and Tiger), insects (Wasp and Hornet), and even weather-related occurrences were the inspiration for some of these nameplates. There was already a Tornado model in the Schwinn line that had sold well as both boys' and girls' bicycles for years. Schwinn's business and marketing management decided to sell another weather-derived model in 1962: the Typhoon. For the Schwinn Company to dub this new model "Typhoon" wasn't really a radical concept, since the Schwinn dealers had been selling the Tornado already. Plus, Schwinn had been using the Typhoon Cord tire for a couple of decades, so the name wasn't a major brainstorm either. The Typhoon bicycle was to be a boys-only model, though, whereas the Tornado was sold in both boys' and girls' versions.

Shown is a typical head badge used on the Typhoons and other middleweights. Here it is seen between the chrome bars of a factory-installed front carrier.

Early in the 1960s, Schwinn executives decided to add another stormy nameplate to the company's model lineup: the Typhoon. Shown here is a 1966 regular model.

The Schwinn Westwind tire was the most common original tire on Typhoons and other middleweights. This 1967 Deluxe came with the Superior whitewalls, however.

As mentioned, the Typhoon Cord tire existed in Schwinn's inventory, but that was an old 2–3/4-inch tire. The new Typhoon was a modern middleweight bicycle with 1-3/4 inch tires; so Typhoons were actually equipped with the smaller Westwind tires, a name connoting a milder weather phenomenon.

For whatever reason, the Schwinn Typhoon model is one of the nameplates that did not span both the heavyweight and middleweight eras. Other models, such as the boys' Panther or the girls' Hollywood, were built during both periods (first as heavyweights, then as middleweights). The Typhoon began production as a middleweight-only version in 1962. In spite of this limitation, however, the Typhoon deserves a little extra attention here. After all, it was the best selling middleweight, and

The classic, twin lower-bar cantilever frame was used on all 20-inch, 24-inch, and 26-inch Typhoon boys' models after 1962.

While Typhoon production continued into the 1980s, the 1962–1969 models are the most collectible. In 1964, a Deluxe version Typhoon was introduced, and this designation was noted on the chain guard.

had the longest middleweight production run (through 1982).

The Typhoon model debuted in 1962, and the serial number was on the left rear dropout bracket until 1970. After 1970, Typhoon production continued, but with changes such as a head tube serial number location; a larger, rectangular rear reflector; additional reflectors; and lower-quality chrome plating. They were even assembled in Greenville, Mississippi, instead of Chicago by 1981, and discontinued in 1983. The later versions simply are not as classic as the earlier ones, because of these changes. Even a small thing like a rear reflector can make a difference; to most collectors, the original round reflector shape has a more timeless appeal. You may think you could change the reflector of the 1970s model to a round one, but it's not that easy. Remember, Schwinn bicycles are dated by serial number, and any change in equipment—no matter how small or insignificant—wouldn't match the model year. Besides, the later model fender has two holes for reflector mounting, and the older fender has only one hole to accept the round reflector. As with all Schwinns, original equipment is most desirable.

Due to the previous reasons, and just plain age, the 1962–1969 models are the best collectibles of the Typhoon series, with a 1962-only straight-bar frame Typhoon being the hardest to find. There were not as many 1962 Typhoons produced, as it was not merely the first year, but the *only* year for this frame on the Typhoon. The introductory model year Typhoons had straight (rather than curved) lower "tank" bars (there was no tank), so the 1962 model is unique within the Typhoon lineage. The straight-bar frame Typhoon was considered a basic or "economy" model, and available only in 1962. The lineup, in typical American fashion; however, quickly expanded to curved lower-bar cantilever frame models, and included Deluxe offerings with available three-speed and hand brake options. In 1962, the Schwinn

The Typhoon colors (except black) were quite iridescent. This 1966 blue model reflects a lot of light for its age.

The Deluxe Typhoon came with a front carrier, larger dual-brace front fender, and whitewall tires. Schwinn also offered an optional three-speed rear hub (as shown on this 1967 model), which required the addition of hand brakes.

This chrome-fendered Deluxe model has a small, round reflector mounted to a chrome bezel that is separate from, but form-fitted to, the fender.

This shiny, chrome front carrier came standard on the Deluxe Typhoons.

Company needed a reason for the Typhoons to be lower priced than other similar models, and they chose to do this with a simpler-in-appearance frame design, even though it wouldn't be any cheaper to produce. Schwinn switched to the ever-popular cantilever frame for the remaining years of the Typhoon (1963 and newer), a move that undoubtedly helped sales. The cantilever frame design has proven its aesthetic appeal continuously since its introduction in 1938 to the present.

Because of the color and option variety available, you will find models from this period with a multitude of equipment combinations and variations. Typhoon color availability varied over the years of the

If you want to make sure that the front carrier is an actual Schwinn part, look closely right here for the SCHWINN name.

model run, with red, as usual for boys' bikes, occupying the top sales spot. Although each year's offerings were slightly different, red, black, blue, green, and gold are the original colors you will find on remaining Typhoons today.

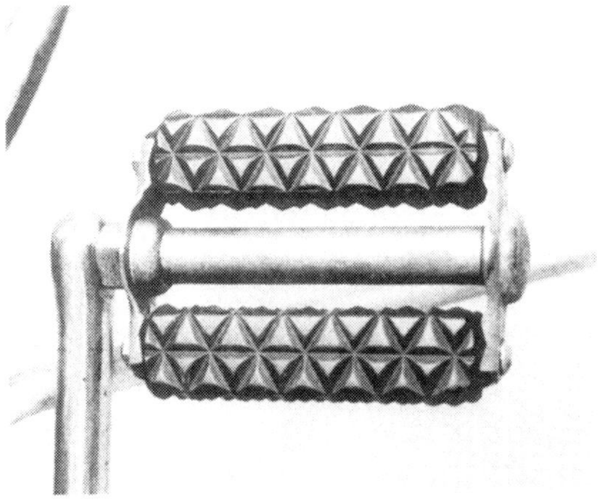

Shown here is the typical Schwinn Approved pedal that was original equipment on standard and Deluxe Typhoons.

One of the great aspects of collecting is how the varied preferences of enthusiasts evenout the market demand. For instance, there are probably just as many collectors who place great value in the standard Typhoons, as those who prefer the Deluxe models. All other things—condition, vintage, and originality—being equal, a loaded model might have a slight edge in value over a plain model, but this is not a steadfast rule. Some collectors specialize in the built-for-function models. Some prefer painted fenders and rims to the chrome-plated alternatives, and vice versa. Earlier models had painted rims and fenders; next, there was a choice of chrome for those parts; and later those parts were available on the Typhoon in chrome only. When the Deluxe Typhoon arrived in 1964, it was noted on the chain guard with a Deluxe Typhoon logo. This version also included a longer leading portion of the front fender, with two sets of braces, a front carrier, a headlight, and whitewall tires.

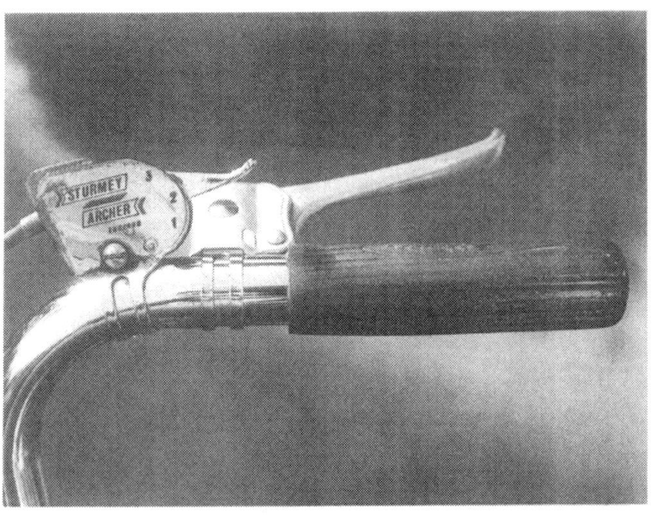

If you ordered a three-speed option on your Deluxe Typhoon, you got a handlebar-mounted British Sturmey-Archer shifter, along with Swiss Weinmann brand hand brakes fore and aft.

Because of the three-speed rear hub option, this 1967 Deluxe Typhoon was equipped with caliper-type hand brakes. An extra frame bracket was welded in place to accommodate the brake caliper mounting on middleweights so equipped.

As usual, vintage (that is, model year) does have an effect on value. In the case of the Typhoons, the 1962-1969 vintages command the most interest and value. The 1970-1979 models have a collector following, but they change hands at a lower value than their older counterparts, even though they look very similar. Like other models built since 1980, the 1980–1982 Typhoons have very little collectibility now, but who knows about the future? If you come upon a near perfect 1982 Typhoon, it might be hard to pass up at a low price.

The coaster brake models used a standard frame with no provision for hand brake caliper mounting.

The front hand brake caliper mounts to the front fork, which is cast especially for this purpose. The fender employs an L-shaped bracket for its upper mount, unlike the coaster brake version.

The coaster brake models have a front fender mounting screw positioned underneath the fender; that screw threads directly into the fork casting.

There are always some aspects of the bicycle models which prompt one to ask, "Why did the manufacturer do this?" The 1969 model year offering, for example, included a regular and a Deluxe Typhoon, and they both came standard with a single-speed coaster brake. When it came to the optional hub, however, the Deluxe was only outfitted with the three-speed, and the popular two-speed automatic kick-back hub was only available on the regular Typhoon. So what did someone who wanted the Deluxe model with the two-speed hub do? Authorized Schwinn dealers were supposed to deliver the bicycles as specified, but there were exceptions. One dealer said that he would ride a bike around the block, so he could call it used, and then equip it any way the customer wanted. In the case of a 1969 Deluxe Typhoon, he would start with a single-speed Deluxe, and change rear rims along with the whitewall tire, to create the two-speed Deluxe, and sell this used non-factory version

The single-speed Typhoon coaster brake models featured an American-built Bendix brand rear hub, which was common on all middleweights.

to the happy buyer. This sort of dealer modification produced many bikes with seemingly original factory setups that really were not from the factory. Collectors argue whether some of these bicycles that were dealer or customer modified with factory parts are really originals. Because decades have passed since these bikes originated, owners, as well as dealers have enjoyed creating their own "customs," taking advantage of the interchangeability of parts among models.

Among the factory-issued model variations, the Deluxe Typhoon, sporting a three-speed rear hub combined with hand-operated caliper-type brakes fore and aft, was the top-of-the-line and therefore most expensive Typhoon. Like automobile manufacturers of today, Schwinn obtained many production parts from foreign sources before the practice was commonplace. The Sturmey-Archer

The Bendix Company also built the automatic two-speed hub, which was introduced in 1960 on the Panther III, and available on Typhoons and other middleweights through 1968. This photo also clearly shows the position of the serial number stamping for middleweight Schwinns.

three-speed hub was of British origin and was installed along with the Swiss-built Weinmann handbrake system. The three-speed model also required a different frame and fork than the one- and two-speed coaster brake models, as to accommodate the caliper installation.

Besides color and option variability, the Typhoon came in three sizes. The big seller was the 26-inch model, but there was a 24-inch and a 20-inch Typhoon to fit smaller riders. For the first-time riders, the 20-inch Typhoon was also listed in the 1969 sales brochure with training wheels for $4 extra. Again, because of diverse collecting interests and habits, enthusiasts seek the smaller Typhoons as fervently as the bigger ones, and certain collectors seek the small ones exclusively.

Some changes occurring in the Typhoon lineup over its run are subtle, but may make a difference to specific collectors. The type of front sprocket used on the Typhoons is an example. Up until 1969, the familiar four-circle and four-triangle stamping was seen on all Typhoons. A "mag" sprocket with five spokes and triangular slots had been a dealer-available accessory in the mid-1960s. In 1969 this mag-type sprocket became standard. As stated earlier, other small changes occurred by the 1970s, including moving the serial

Up until 1969, this familiar circle-and-triangle sprocket was standard on the Typhoon series and other middleweights.

The adjustable control cable moves the internal gear mechanism on this Sturmey-Archer three-speed rear hub.

In 1969, Schwinn began installing this mag-type sprocket on the Typhoons and other models.

number to the head tube; adding reflectors to the spokes, pedals, and handlebars; and the appearance of a large, rectangular rear fender reflector. As these modern improvements took place, the classic appeal began to diminish.

Whenever you can find a complete, original bike, it is certainly most preferable, but it's not that easy. For example, very few models from the 1960s that originally came with handlebar-mounted headlights had them for long because of their vulnerability to damage. With this in mind, don't overlook a nice bike with a few missing parts, as you can search for and find these parts separately, and in the case of the Typhoon, without much difficulty.

Because the Typhoon was such a strong seller, a good supply still remains today. Because of its classic design, rugged construction, and great ride, the Typhoon definitely has the timeless physical and aesthetic qualities to fit the term "classic."

Tornado

The Tornado was conceived as an economy model for the 1958 model year, and carried the lowest price in the line at $39.95. This bottom-of-the-line status gives the Tornado a distinction that creates interest with collectors today.

In keeping with its economy image, the Tornado had painted fenders and rims and was only available with a one-speed coaster brake hub. The Tornado was sold in both boys' and girls' models, but colors were restricted to red for boys and blue for girls. During its model-year run from 1958 through 1961, the Tornado could be purchased in 20-, 24-, or 26-inch sizes.

To differentiate this economy line, Schwinn used a slightly modified cantilever frame for the boys' bikes. The two side-by-side lower bars on the frame were straight rather than curved, and do not connect to the rear frame bars at the seat tube as they do on the normal cantilever design. Typically,

The boys' Tornados used this unique, straight-bar frame, and were considered economy models. This 1962 model is in virtually unused condition.

obscure features such as this create additional mystique and increased classic appeal for bicycles. Also in keeping with its economy image, the Tornado models used a bolt-on kickstand in place of the Schwinn-famous built-in kickstand.

In 1959, Schwinn decided to bring a Deluxe Tornado to the marketplace. They accomplished this with the addition of a tank, light, rack, and a $10 price increase to the basic Tornado. The Deluxe Tornado still

This 1961 girls' Tornado is mainly utilitarian in design, but it is just as rugged and dependable as any Schwinn.

had a one-speed hub, so if you find any Tornado bicycles with multiple speeds, they were added after production. The basic and deluxe versions were sold in both boys' and girls' types, and both 26- and 24-inch sizes through 1961, after which Tornados were discontinued. The 20-inch juvenile model was only offered as a standard Tornado throughout the model run. As with other middleweights produced before 1970, the serial number is on the frame by the left rear axle dropout, and referencing the number will allow you to determine the year of the frame production.

The Schwinn Tornado was billed in Schwinn literature as "America's whirlwind bike value!" and a model that "offers all the

Throughout the 1950s and 1960s, each and every model had its own unique logo silk-screened on its chain guard.

Some economy models, like this 1961 Tornado, used a bolt-on kickstand well after 1946, the year that the built-in type was introduced.

famous Schwinn quality features at a special low, low price!" Because of their limited model years and low-end status, the Tornado bicycles are great classic finds today. They will never reach the value of some of the more equipped middleweights like Jaguars and Corvettes, but a nice Deluxe Tornado would come close, and be even a little more unique.

Hollywood

The Schwinn Hollywood, exclusively a girls' model, made its debut in 1938 as a heavyweight, equipped, balloon-tire bicycle. The middleweight Hollywood that came to market in 1957 was listed in the dealer catalog as unequipped. Nevertheless, advertising copy from the era stated, "You'll find all the excitement of a Hollywood movie set in the easy-handling Schwinn Hollywood model!"

The middleweight Hollywoods were not like their well-equipped heavyweight sisters, but this 1967 model with whitewalls, chrome fenders, and chrome rims still casts a striking image. This one is also equipped with a Schwinn Approved speedometer from the same year.

This 24-inch 1958 Hollywood has a more classic look because of its painted fenders. The color scheme on this one is radiant blue and white.

Evidently the Schwinn marketing department believed that the association with California's Hollywood was a powerful one for girls. This theory was also at play with other models like the Starlet and Debutante.

Even though the middleweight Hollywood was not a deluxe bike, it did come with some new colors. In addition to the typical color options of radiant blue and radiant red, buyers could choose two-tone treatments of summer cloud white and holiday rose, or summer cloud white and powder blue. Paint schemes of this type are an example of the atypical features that help create classic appeal.

Throughout the 1960s, the Hollywood was the best girls' middleweight seller. Without explanation, Hollywood models did not appear in the 1961 catalog, but they reappeared in 1962 and remained through 1982. Therefore, the Hollywood was offered longer than any other girls' middleweight, and many examples remain today. Since the Hollywood spanned so many years, it was affected by the serial number location change in 1970. The bikes through 1969 had their serial numbers stamped by the left rear axle dropout, but beginning with 1970, the numbers were stamped on the head tube, below the Schwinn badge. The production year is coded within these numbers.

As with the Typhoon, when models like the Hollywood passed 1970, some of their classic appeal began to diminish. Factors that played a role in this phenomenon included larger, reshaped rear reflectors; additional

The Hollywoods stayed in the middleweight lineup longer than any girls' models, until 1982. This 1980 Hollywood shows the different and additional reflectors that were attached beginning in the 1970s. The rear baskets are an add-on accessory.

reflectors on pedals, wheels, and stem; different cranks and sprockets; and supplier and production changes. This is not to say that no one will consider the post-1969 models as classics, but they are certainly less classic than the older ones. Part of this situation is due to age difference between the two eras, and part is due to character change with the newer versions.

Beginning with its middleweight introductory year of 1957, the Hollywood was built in 26-, 24-, and 20-inch models. In 1965, a Deluxe Hollywood arrived in dealers' showrooms complete with a front rack, headlight, and whitewall tires. The Deluxe Hollywood remained until 1969, and from 1970 through 1982 you could only get a standard Hollywood. Another change for the Hollywood and all other middleweights came in 1972, when the 24-inch sizes were eliminated, and only one adult size, 26-inch, and one juvenile size, 20-inch, remained available.

The same things that made the Schwinn Hollywood popular in the past still make it very appealing today. The name, the quality, the colors, and the affordability are all positive characteristics that have held value over the years and lure collectors now. Two of the main factors that make the Hollywood series fun to seek are its availability and lowprice. Also, even if a Hollywood is incomplete or in rough condition, it still has value, because most of its parts fit all the other middleweights.

The Debutante was the girls' Corvette or Jaguar. This 1961 model shows how well equipped they were. This example still has its headlight, along with other choice goodies like a horn tank, front and rear racks, teardrop reflector, and whitewall tires.

Debutante

When the girls' Corvette model was discontinued in 1959, it did not end the production of equipped girls' models. Schwinn proved this with the introduction of the Debutante in 1959. Advertising for the Debutante told the girls that it was "All new... and just for you!" The name alone suggested that this was a bicycle for girls, since a debutante is a young woman making her official debut in society. Apparently, Schwinn hoped to convince girls that owning a Schwinn Debutante was a good way to make a social debut, or begin a career.

Since it is a deluxe, equipped bicycle, the seat tube decal on this 1961 Debutante is of the ornate variety.

As Schwinn advertising stated, the Debutante bicycle would cause a flashy debut of its own: "Its features are fashioned to steal the show wherever you go!" Features of the Debutante included twin headlights, slimline tank with horn, front and rear carriers, two-tone saddle, and whitewall tires. As a premium model, the Debutante also carried the ornate seat down tube decal, the teardrop-shaped rear reflector, and two-tone paint options.

The Debutante was a bicycle with a fairly short production run, since it was discontinued after the 1962 edition. All of the Debutantes were full-sized, 26-inch models, and the serial numbers were stamped at the left rear dropouts. In 1959 and 1960, the Debutantes were only available with a one-speed hub. For 1961 and 1962, the two-speed automatic and three-speed cable-operated hubs were added.

As previously mentioned, girls' bikes occupy a lower rung on the classic ladder, but premium models like the Debutante certainly must not be overlooked. The frame style might be secondary to the boys' cantilever design, but a two-speed, two-tone Debutante with all of its original features would hold its own at any vintage bicycle display.

Fair Lady

Nearly a twin sister to the Debutante, the Schwinn Fair Lady was also introduced in 1959. The Fair Lady was considered a top-of-the-line equipped bicycle, very similar to the Debutante. The Fair Lady was even

Fair Lady bikes, like this 1961 example, were considered premium bikes. The front rack, sport pedals, deluxe chain guard, and deluxe seat were all standard issue.

Above: Once again, the name that is silk-screened on the chain guard is artwork unique to this model.

Left: Typical of premium middleweights, the "Quality Seal" is integral to the design of the elaborate pinstripe decal on this 1961 Fair Lady.

priced a few dollars higher, due to its standard three-speed hub (one- and two-speeds optional), and stainless steel fenders. The name inference suggested that this model was for a "fair lady," and Schwinn promised via their ads that the Fair Lady owner would "Ride like a Queen!"

Fair Lady models are fairly rare, since they were made for only three years: 1959, 1960, and 1961. The name did reappear as a Sting-Ray model in 1964, which is discussed in the next chapter. The rarest Fair Lady would have to be a 1959 24-inch version,

The deluxe seat on the Fair Lady has a chrome crash bar and chrome springs. It's nice to find them in this condition today.

since that is the only year that size was manufactured. The size for all of the other Fair Lady models was 26-inch. All of the serial number stampings are on the frames at the left rear dropout position. Colors offered on the Fair Lady were red, blue, green, or black.

The Fair Lady has classic appeal due to its limited production, solid quality, and nifty accessories. Even though they are rare, it might be easier to find a nice Fair Lady than a Corvette or Jaguar, because girls generally took better care of their bikes and rode them less than boys did.

Co-Ed

The Schwinn Co-Ed is a basic, unequipped girls' middleweight model that you could buy from 1960 through 1964. It had all of

This 1960 Co-Ed is in the middle of the model stratification. It has chrome rims, but painted fenders and no accessories. The owner added the whitewalls.

The lettering for the Co-Ed logo has a bold, simple design that makes it unique.

Schwinn's quality features, but it did not have many accessories. Sometimes it is a very small feature that adds classical appeal, however, and in the case of the Co-Ed, it is simply the name, and the way it is written.

The name was probably a sign of the times, when increasing numbers of women were going to college. For many girls, the dainty, glamorous images portrayed by the Starlet, Fair Lady, or Debutante were outdated. The Co-Ed portrayed a more practical, all-business image. In contrast to how Co-Ed is written, most model names appear as a logo in stylish script, or stylized print on chain guards and in advertisements. The stark, bold, block-letter design of the Co-Ed logo is in great contrast to the lavish script of the Debutante or Fair Lady. Even other models with block printing have the letters puffed-up or styled in some other way. The lettering of the Co-Ed logo is leaning forward a bit, and does have small serifs, but its bold, almost brash look really stands out. This characteristic, which is a departure from the norm, adds a certain unique mystique.

The Co-Ed was available in 24-inch and 26-inch sizes, except in 1962, when the 24-inch model was not available; it's just another one of those factory anomalies. The Co-Ed, like other middleweights before 1960, had the serial number stamped on the frame by the left rear dropout. This model is certainly not at the top of any classic listing, but its name and logo are a standout.

Starlet, Starlet II, and Starlet III

For those girls who were not so practical, the equipped Starlet series endured. For star struck females, the middleweight Starlet (previously a balloon-tire heavyweight) was available from 1957 through 1970. The

This 1966 Starlet III is another example of an equipped middleweight. The racks, tank, chrome, and whitewalls give these bikes their premium stature. If the paint was not faded, "Starlet III" would be visible on the chain guard.

Starlet changed to Starlet II in 1965, and then to Starlet III in 1966. This Roman numeral series is another example of how a model name is actually a classic feature.

In the case of the Starlet series, however, a lot of other classic features graced all of the models. Deluxe horn tanks, headlights, chrome rims, racks, and whitewall tires were all found on these premium girls' bicycles. Additionally, you could have two-tone paint schemes of Summer Cloud White and Rose, or Summer Cloud White and Powder Blue on your Starlet. The II and III models had even more chrome and were available in radiant violet, blue, and green.

During the Starlet production, all of the sizes (20, 24, 26) were represented, but not every size, every year; as usual, the whims of Schwinn were at play. Starlets were offered with all three rear hub variations (one, two, three), and all of their serial numbers are where you would expect, by the rear axle dropout.

As usual, not as many collectors are looking for a Starlet as compared to those seeking a Jaguar or Corvette. Like the Debutante and Fair Lady, however, the Starlet models have the unique qualities of name, colors, and a long list of accessories to justify a position among the other classic Schwinns.

The slimline tank on this 1966 Starlet III has a built-in horn (notice button).

Other Middleweights

The preceding listings represent the best-selling popular middleweights sold by Schwinn from 1955 through 1982, but there are a few others. These other models are all very similar to the middleweights previously described, but the names are different. Some other boys' middleweights you will find are: Fleet, Flying Star, Heavy-Duti, Hornet, Speedster, Skipper, and a 20-inch Buddy. Other model names for girls' middleweights are: Catalina, Fiesta, Debbie, Candy, and a 20-inch Barbie. Another fine classic unequipped middleweight you will surely see is the Schwinn Spitfire; it was available in both boys' and girls' models. Last, and certainly not least, is the Bantam. That bicycle will get another mention in Chapter 9, and is distinctive mainly because it was the last middleweight model, and had

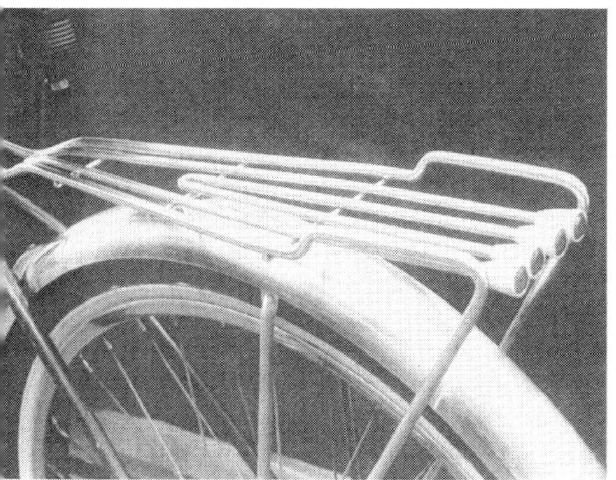

The Starlet I, II, and III all used this Schwinn rack with four reflectors and cool, built-in fins.

Schwinn had a lot of names on the middleweight roster, and the Hornet model name was one that was revived from the heavyweight era. This 1963 chain guard shows how the silk-screened lettering fades away after years of exposure.

Middleweights other than the ones mentioned elsewhere in this chapter are similar bikes with different names; the Spitfire is an example of this. The name on the chain guard of this boys' 1957 model is fading as usual; it is actually a Deluxe Spitfire, because of the chrome rims.

one of the longest middleweight production runs (1960 through 1985). The Bantam was known as a "convertible" because it had a removable top-bar, which made it suitable for either boys or girls.

The Schwinn middleweight line accounted for a large portion of Schwinn's history and success through the 1950s and 1960s. Their popularity waned in the second half of the 1960s, as they had to compete with the Sting-Rays and 10-speed bicycles. They were the bikes for the masses in their day because of their quality, style, features, and function. As these bicycles get harder to find, those qualities, along with their extremely satisfying ride, will make them even more desirable.

The equipped, premium models like the Jaguars and Corvettes were the undisputed stars of the middleweight line, but the bread-and-butter models like the Typhoons and Hollywoods sold in big numbers. In the end, those latter two models were the only two full-sized middleweights in the Schwinn catalog from 1971-1982.

The Cruiser was to be the next use of the tried-and-true cantilever frame. With Sting-Rays and 10-speeds bringing middleweight

This common graphic treatment was for unequipped middleweights of the 1950s and early 1960s. It is shown here on a 1958 Spitfire, along with the ever-present and ever-popular cantilever frame.

sales to a halt, the days of the middleweights were numbered. In 1980, Schwinn began making the Cruiser models, and by 1983 they stopped making middleweights entirely. The Cruiser models were basically middleweight bikes without fenders, but they sported the 2.125-inch tire from the balloon-tire era. The Cruiser line sold fairly well over the next several decades in many variations (see Chapter 8).

The middleweight Schwinns have a solid position in the classic Schwinn hierarchy. Their numbers are still plentiful, and they are still a relative bargain in the collector marketplace. They are easy to work on, original parts availability is good, and many suppliers now offer reproduction parts. These are all characteristics that make collecting the middleweights a lot of fun. Now go out and see what you can buy!

Chapter 5

Classic Schwinn Sting-Rays

★★★½	Sting-Ray 1963–1/2–1969
★★½	Sting-Ray 1970 and later
★★★★	Super Deluxe Sting-Ray
★★★★½	Krate series
★★★	Other Sting-Ray models

Schwinn Sting-Ray bicycles, in all of their "way cool" variations, occupy a prominent position in bicycle history. They ranked as a true marketing phenomenon when they first arrived in 1963, and they represent one of the largest segments of the vintage bicycle hobby today. It is truly amazing that, in terms of current collector interest and value, they stand about equal to many classic Schwinns that are 30 to 40 years older!

After their mid-year introduction in 1963–1/2, Sting-Rays kept getting cooler all the time. The many features of these newly styled little bikes reached out and grabbed

Schwinn introduced the first Sting-Rays in 1963–1/2. In 1964 they developed the Super Deluxe versions with whitewalls and spring forks, like the 1966 model seen here.

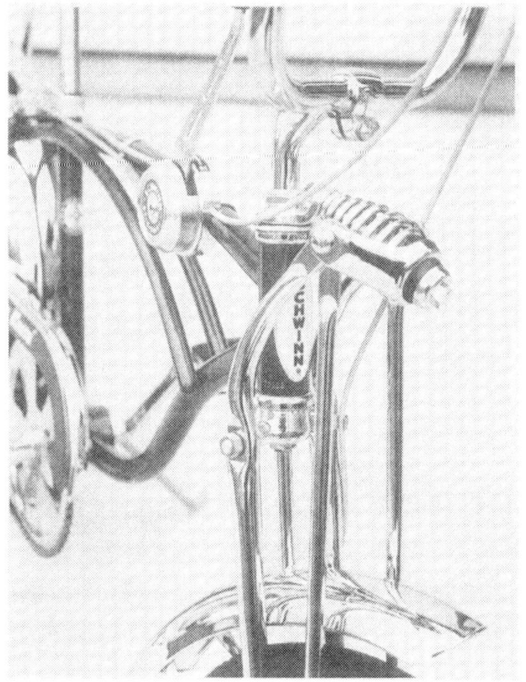

Above: Bicycle manufacturers were first alerted to the muscle bike phenomenon when kids in California began altering 20-inch bicycles. They were attaching "banana" or "polo" seats and high-rise handlebars to regular bikes, creating predecessors to the Sting-Rays. This 1961 Tornado was modified in 1964, which was just after the Sting-Rays hit the market.

Left: The Krate series (1968–1973) showcased all the tricks that Schwinn engineers had up their sleeves. Shown on this 1970 Apple Krate are a few features that help make these bikes top classics: the 1938-style spring fork, the five-speed Stik-Shift (as Schwinn spelled it), and a shorty front fender over a 16-inch front wheel.

buyers. Based on a 20-inch juvenile bike, even the standard Sting-Ray had a special look, with its polo seat and high-rise handlebars, which had not been seen previously on a factory-produced bicycle. When the Super Deluxe Sting-Ray arrived to market in 1964 sporting whitewall tires and a spring-fork, it seemed like the ultimate classic. It was not the pinnacle, though, because the Krate series Sting-Rays beginning in 1968 outmuscled all of the muscle bikes.

The reason for the immediate success of the Sting-Ray was that the market was primed for the new bicycle before its introduction. The buyers were waiting for the product, and someone just needed to manufacture it. Imaginative youths in California were creating custom bicycles during the early 1960s by affixing banana seats and high-rise handlebars to 20-inch bicycles. Actually, the seat was a polo design made by the oldest bicycle seat company: Persons. The seats had not initially met with market approval, and they were sitting all over California in excess inventory. It was a sudden high demand for, and shortage of, 20-inch frames that first alerted retailers to the events taking place. After some investigation, Schwinn's Al Fritz found out what was happening. From those lessons, he developed a prototype Schwinn that he soon dubbed Sting-Ray.

It seems mere fate that Al Fritz and Schwinn were the ones to seize this market opportunity; all the cards simply fell into place to make it happen. It was rumored at the time that the Huffman Corporation had some prototypes ready to go, so timing would be crucial. In spite of initial resistance, Schwinn retailers and executives

There were changes coming yearly in the Sting-Ray line. One of the items offered beginning in 1965 was the Schwinn Slik, furthering the image association with drag racing. Here a 1970 Cotton Picker shows off this cool tire.

decided that the Sting-Ray was a "fun little bike," and gave the project a green light. The rest is history. After its 1963–1/2 introduction, Schwinn sold all of the Sting-Rays that they could produce before the end of the year, and a whole bunch more during the ensuing decade. At a time when Schwinn considered 10,000 annual sales of any single model to be a good result, the Sting-Ray's first-year sales of 45,000 units was quite a feat.

The first Schwinn Sting-Rays were basic 20-inch bicycles with a polo seat and high handlebars; they didn't even have fenders. What they did have was the name, the look, and the timing to captivate the youth market. Their hot rod-like "big and little" approach to tires (2.125-inch rear and 1–3/4 inch front), along with the custom seat and handlebars lent an aggressive, all-business image to the new "lean and mean" bicycles. This image was similar to the one portrayed by the muscle cars that were introduced at about the same time. The Sting-Rays used a familiar brick-tread Westwind tire up front, but they had a new, wider studded rear tire. "Studded" referred to a bumpy or knobby type of tread, not to metal studs as in the automotive world. The studded-style tread was an early version of an off-road BMX or mountain bike tread.

The colors offered for the first model year were Flamboyant Red, Flamboyant Lime, and Radiant Coppertone. The rims for the Sting-Ray were components from past models: the rear S-2 rim came from the balloon-tire 20-inch juvenile bikes, and the front S-7 rim was from the 20-inch middleweights. The 1963 and 1964 models had 36 spokes, while later model years used only 28 spokes. You must count the holes before interchanging rims and hubs to be certain that they match up.

The serial numbers for all of the Sting-Rays built before 1970 are stamped on the frame near the left rear axle dropout; on 1970 and later models, the number is stamped on the head tube below the Schwinn oval badge. These numbers designate the year of individual frame production, not necessarily the catalog year. The early Sting-Rays were all the same size. All had boys' cantilever frames, and all had one-speed Bendix rear hubs.

As with automobile marketing, the simpler introductory model Sting-Rays were soon joined by new and improved offerings. The very next year, 1964, Schwinn introduced two new models and some extra color choices. As an alternative to the standard Sting-Ray, you could now buy a Deluxe Sting-Ray, which featured a deluxe saddle, chrome fenders, and whitewall

The Super Deluxe Sting-Rays were so designated on their chromed and painted chain guards. As on other Sting-Rays, this artwork was silk-screened at the factory. Now, decals are available, but Hyper-Formance (see resources at this book's end) screens them just like originals.

tires. Girls could opt for a step-through frame model named the Fair Lady. Sky blue and violet were added to the red, lime, and gold (Coppertone) color choices for the Sting-Rays in 1964. The Fair Lady was available in blue, violet, or a two-tone white and rose. One advertisement from 1964 mentions that the Fair Lady comes "with an attractive floral decorated basket," somewhat softening the bike's image; tomboys could always detach the basket if they wanted a tougher look.

There were a lot of changes announced for the 1965 Sting-Ray lineup; one of the coolest was the Schwinn Slik rear tire. As Schwinn promotional literature described it, it had "More road surface than any other bike tire. You've seen them on drag racers and track cars—now available for the first time on bikes." Even the standard Sting-Rays were equipped with this tire, and the standard models could also be ordered with one-, two-, or three-speed rear hubs. The two-speed was a Bendix Automatic Overdrive unit, and the three-speed was a Sturmey-Archer cable-operated hub. The Deluxe Sting-Rays for 1965 offered all three of the hub options, but came with a studded whitewall tire instead of the Schwinn Slik. The engineering department had at least one more trick still up its collective sleeve: the Super Deluxe Sting-Ray. This new model could have either a studded or Slik rear tire and a one- or two-speed hub, but included a blast from the past: the famous 1938-design spring fork in a dazzling all-chrome version. This mix of old and new is a prime example of how Schwinn had a way of creating classic bicycles.

In 1966 the Sting-Ray Fastback model brought the five-speed derailleur to the lineup, along with the Stik-Shift. There was more to this bike than an added shifter, however. The frame wasn't cantilever design, but rather a unique 20-inch modified lightweight frame with a curved top bar. The one pictured here is a 1968 model.

The seat tube decal on this 1968 Fastback is the same as the ones used on chain guards of 1961 and 1962 five-speed Corvettes.

For the 1966 models, the Sting-Ray family was still in the expansion mode. Certain changes were subtle. The Super Deluxe now came with a studded tire (no Slik was offered), and the Flamboyant Lime color choice disappeared. Other changes were not so subtle. One of the standard models had an available top-bar mounted stick-shift control for the three-speed option, and a sportier girls' model, the Slik-Chik, was offered. A Junior Sting-Ray, with lower handlebars and 1-3/4 inch tires on *both* the front and rear, joined the lineup along with a girls' counterpart, the Lil Chik.

Another drastic departure from the norm was the introduction of the Fastback Sting-Ray in 1966. This new model introduced the five-sprocket freewheeling rear gear cluster to the Sting-Ray line. The derailleur mechanism was controlled with a top-bar-mounted stick shift (Schwinn called it a Stik Shift) that emulated an automobile floor-shift. This was still a 20-inch model, but was equipped with narrower 1–3/8-inch tires; it also sported a mag-type sprocket, and was available in black, along with gold, violet, and blue. It is suspected that the idea

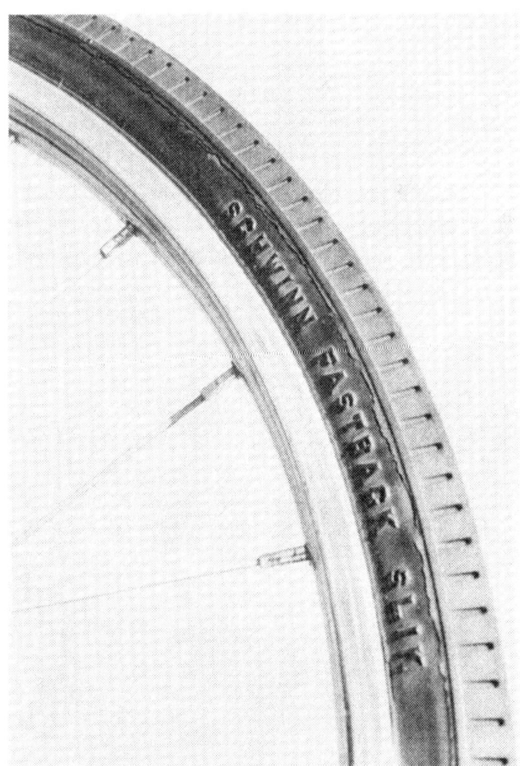

The Fastback series had its own Slik tire, as shown here, with the name molded in; it was 1 3/8-inches wide.

For 1967 Schwinn came up with the Ram's Horn Fastbacks. They were like the other Fastbacks, with the addition of the curly handlebars shown on this 1968 bicycle. The last year to feature this model was 1968, so for only two years these handlebars were made.

for the Fastback was born in a California bicycle shop out of a desire to create a lighter, faster, multi-speed Sting-Ray. For Schwinn's part, it was once again Al Fritz who was running with these ideas to create new models. As Fritz explained, "We took a 20-inch diamond frame, which is a lightweight style, and named it the Fastback. We curved the top bar. That's where we got the name Fastback because it was more of a touring type of bicycle. It just made sense to us."

The ram's horn artwork is still visible on the chain guard of this 1968 Ram's Horn Fastback, and obviously is exclusive to this marque.

The Midget Sting-Rays were produced from 1967 through 1972. Like the 1970 bicycle shown here, Midgets had a scaled down cantilever frame and smaller 16-inch wheels.

Another Sting-Ray anomaly is this Pixie II from the 1980s. It doesn't use a cantilever frame, but it does say Sting-Ray on the chain guard.

Around 1967, Schwinn wanted to associate much of the lineup with Sting-Rays. These Lil Tigers were built from 1967 through 1980, and had 12-inch wheels with solid rubber tires. They emulated Sting-Rays because of their polo seats and high handlebars. This one is equipped with Schwinn Cycle Aids—another name for training wheels.

The Fastback was a decent seller, and remained in the catalog through 1976. A close cousin to the Fastback was the Ram's Horn Fastback Sting-Ray, which was exactly like a regular Fastback, except it had some outrageous handlebars that were designed after the curly horns of a ram. The Ram's Horn edition, which appeared in 1967, never sold well and was discontinued in 1968. This short model run, not to mention its obscure appearance, makes for a cult-type following of the Ram's Horn models today.

Besides the Ram's Horn Fastback, the Midget Sting-Rays came to market in 1967 as well. What Schwinn described as a "miniature version of the popular Sting-Ray," the Midget had smaller 16-inch wheels and a scaled down frame. It was a basic coaster brake model without fenders, but it offered the coolness of the Sting-Ray to even younger riders than before. The Lil Tiger was introduced in 1967 also; it could loosely be called a Sting-Ray because of its polo seat. It was a model suited for the tiny tykes, with

The Lil Tigers had nifty artwork on their chain guards, but the "no brakes" warning was a little bit unnerving.

hard rubber airless tires and a fixed (no brakes) rear hub. The Lil Tiger remained in the Schwinn product line through 1980.

Next came 1968 (drum roll please), and the introduction of the legendary Sting-Ray Krate Series. As Schwinn put it, "A whole new world of cycling thrills can be yours when you blast off and move out aboard the flashiest Sting-Rays ever designed." According to Schwinn price and catalog literature, the only Krate offered in 1968 was the Orange Krate; it was a good one to open with, as it

The Orange Krate kicked off the Krate series in 1968. This most successful Krate model was painted in Kool Orange and had plenty of equipment, as is the case with the 1972 bike shown here.

The Stik-Shift appeared on all derailleur-equipped Krates. It was exactly like the Fastback shifter, but somehow it looked better attached to a Krate's cantilever frame. Consumer safety groups eventually halted production of this shifter, but not before millions of classic Krates were created.

remained the top-selling Krate in most regions for the next six years. As with all top classic bicycles, special and plentiful extras were the order of the day. The Orange Krate borrowed one such feature from the Super Deluxe Sting-Ray, which borrowed it from the balloon-tire bikes: the front spring fork. The Orange Krate, like the rest of the Krates to come, had a host of other new and exciting features, too. For starters, the color, Kool Orange, was new and very well suited for a muscle bike. Spring struts on the seat added a cushioned ride. The front wheel was downsized to 16 inches and incorporated a heavy-duty aluminum-housed drum brake. The way-cool Schwinn five-speed Stik-Shift controlled the freewheeling rear derailleur setup, and the rear brakes were hand-operated caliper-types. Plentiful extras? A resounding "yes!"

By 1969, Schwinn was proud of the Sting-Ray and Krate lineup. That year, they offered three additional Krates: The Apple Krate (Flamboyant Red), the Lemon Peeler (Kool Lemon), and the Pea Picker (Campus

The short fender, the aluminum-housed drum brake, and the smaller 16-inch front wheel added to the custom look of the Krate models.

The second Krate, the Apple Krate, was introduced in 1969. Like all Apple Krates, this 1970 model was painted Flamboyant Red. All of the Krates had seats to match their paint.

Green). Whereas the 1968 Orange Krates came with a studded tire, the 1969 models were introduced with a Color-Line Gripper-Slik, which reverted to a black Slik the following years. A 1969 Schwinn sales brochure titled, "Schwinn Sting-Ray...The Bike That Changed Cycling," described the bike:

> Sting-Ray, known as the "bike with the sports car look," has revolutionized cycling since its introduction by Schwinn in 1963. It has won the praise and captured the imagination of youngsters of all ages across the U.S.A. This is the fun bike that features a short frame, high rise handlebars and long, bucket shaped saddle. This design gives the rider an exciting combination of features for quick maneuvers, fast starts and short radius turns. A lightweight version of the Sting-Ray, called the Fastback was introduced in 1966 and quickly became a best seller. This is the 5-speed model that combines the easy pedaling of a lightweight with the maneuverability of the original Sting-Ray. It also achieves an added thrill with the addition of 5-speed gears and

a fast acting Stik-Shift gear shifter. For distance rides, short hops, or for just plain riding fun, the Schwinn Fastback is great. In 1968, Schwinn opened up a new field of cycling enjoyment with the unveiling of the revolutionary designed Orange Krate Sting-Ray. In just a year this exiting five-speed Stik-Shift model has become the most talked about Sting-Ray in bikedom. This year, there are four hot color versions of the Krate to choose from. Schwinn Krate models feature the combination of a 20-inch rear wheel with a 16-inch front wheel, with styling similar to the racing cars found on drag racing tracks.

Yes, that shows Schwinn was proud, but not necessarily complacent. In 1970, they offered yet another Krate: the Cotton Picker in plain white (not Kool or Flamboyant). That year, Schwinn also let you buy the Krate bikes with a one-speed coaster brake hub. The purpose for this was most likely to gain a bigger market share, since the nearly $100 price tag on the shifter bikes was considered very expensive; the coaster brake model was almost $20 less. The Cotton Picker never sold that well and only lasted for two model years, 1970 and 1971. The serial numbers for Cotton Pickers are stamped on the head tube by the Schwinn badge.

When it comes to classic cool, it is hard to beat the look of the freewheeling five-speed gear cluster and derailleur attached to a 20-inch cantilever frame. Also visible on this 1970 Apple Krate are other great features like the Mag front sprocket (slightly different from middleweight and lightweight mag-type sprockets), lower seat strut shocks, sport pedals, and caliper brakes.

The cool Krate features were seemingly endless, as evidenced by the seat's racing stripe and the bobbed rear fender treatment seen here.

Top: The Lemon Peeler also had a 1969 introduction, and its color was in character, Kool Lemon. The model shown here is from 1973, the final year of production.

Bottom: For 1969, if you didn't like orange, red, or yellow, you could also get a green Krate model: the Pea Picker. The 1972 model shown here was officially painted in Campus Green.

Top: In 1970, Schwinn had some more ideas, which they showed by introducing the Cotton Picker Krate model. The Cotton Pickers were finished in plain white and never sold that well. They were only built in 1970 and 1971, so examples like this 1970 model are hard to find now.

Bottom: The most rare Schwinn Krate is probably the Grey Ghost. It was painted Silver Mist Grey, and was not a huge seller. Low sales, combined with a one-year-only production, make sightings like this 1971 model very rare.

Krate models like the six seen here—the Lemon Peeler, the Grey Ghost, the Pea Picker, the Orange Krate, the Apple Krate, and the Cotton Picker—made their way into millions of homes across America from 1968 to 1973. Now, they seem to be doing it all over again.

The Krate series lasted six years, and consisted of six models. Mentioned so far are the Orange Krate, the Apple Krate, the Lemon Peeler, the Pea Picker, and the Cotton Picker. That leaves one more to make six, and that is the elusive Grey Ghost. It is elusive not because of its name, but because it appeared in the catalog for only one year, 1971. The Grey Ghost was like the other Krates, except, of course, it sported its own color: Silver Mist Grey. It was an attractive bicycle with its metallic gray (Schwinn spelled it "grey") paint and black accents. Maybe it wasn't that popular in 1971, but today, due to its rarity, the Grey Ghost is highly sought after by collectors.

Even with the later-model Krates, Schwinn was innovating. The standout feature for 1972 was an available rear disc brake. A feature borrowed from the automobile and motorcycle industry, the disc brake looked right at home on the Krate bicycles. Today, the value of a disc brake by itself exceeds the price of the original bikes threefold. Like many of the quirky features found on the Krates, the rear disc brake was bound to create eventual classic status for the bikes they adorned.

It seems that all good things must come to an end, and so it was for the Krate bikes. Sales must have been slipping a bit, because by 1973, only the Orange Krate, the Apple

Krate, and the Lemon Peeler remained. The Consumer Product Safety Commission delivered a serious blow in 1974, when they banned all bar-mounted bicycle stick shifts from production. This took away one of the coolest elements from these bikes, and in 1974, the Krates were strictly history. Kids

Right: If you can find one of these Krate disc brake setups, you will have something of good value—currently nearly $500. This super cool automotive-type feature was available as an option on 1972 and 1973 Krates.

Below: As some of the Krate fervor was dwindling, Schwinn made an odd attempt to appeal to the older crowd with a 24-inch Manta-Ray in 1971. The tire size for this unusual bike was 24 x 1-3/8 inches. The 1971 yellow Manta-Ray shown here is all-original; the Wald front rack was dealer-installed upon initial delivery.

The extra-wide Manta-Ray seats were designed for additional comfort over the narrow Sting-Ray seats. The Manta-Ray experiment didn't last long, however, as the only years of production were 1971 and 1972.

were buying 10-speed and BMX bikes by 1974, so the glory days of the Krates were fading at that time anyway.

There are some other interesting Sting-Rays that haven't been mentioned yet. The Manta-Ray is now, and probably was then, considered by most people to be a little weird looking. It debuted in 1971 and bowed out of the lineup in 1972. The limited production makes for a cult following, but it's one of those that you either love or hate. The colors for both years were yellow, green, and orange. For 1971 only, Silver Mist Grey was available, probably making that version the most rare. You could have a disc brake on the Manta-Ray too, so for Manta-Ray lovers, a gray one with a disc brake would be the Holy Grail.

Another rare gem from the Sting-Ray series was the one-year-only 1968 Schwinn Sting-Ray Mini-Twinn. This was a tandem Sting-Ray, hard to find back then, and even scarcer today. During the later years of production, Schwinn also came up with a patriotic, bicentennial edition in 1976. This was the only white Sting-Ray besides the Cotton Picker, but it was pretty plain, despite some red and blue accents; it did not sell well in 1973, and doesn't generate a lot of interest yet. There is even an urban legend that Schwinn produced two promotional models named the Koal Krate and the Grape Krate. These are rumored to have black (Koal) and purple (Grape) paint finishes. The only problem with this legend is that no one has been able to produce a bike to bring truth to the rumor. Undoubtedly, someone has re-created these bikes by now, but factory-produced versions have never been documented.

All of the Sting-Rays have to be considered classic Schwinns, with the Krates being super-classics. As with middleweight models, though, Sting-Rays (not Krates) remained in the catalog through 1982, and the later models don't generate the same classic interest as the earlier ones at this time. The interesting thing about Sting-Rays as collectibles is that they are desirable and valuable, but not that scarce. This contradicts conventional wisdom, where the most sought-after items are usually somewhat rare. We know the phenomenon is still alive and well, as many reproduction parts are now available, and there are businesses such as Pete Aronson's Hyper-Formance that specialize in Sting-Rays. The fact that Sting-Rays are relatively plentiful is one factor creating the big following that they currently enjoy. The other factor is that they are great looking, fun bicycles that captivated nearly the entire market in the past; those same qualities are creating that same captivation all over again now.

Chapter 6

Special Classic Schwinns

★★★★★	Whizzer
★★★★	Cycle Truck
★★★★★	Power Cycle Truck
★★★★	Run-A-Bout
★★★	Tandems

Listing every classic Schwinn bicycle is a daunting task, and undoubtedly some classic candidates will elude this text. There are many Schwinn models that were not in the mainstream, but were special in their own way and must be acknowledged here. The following Schwinns, while not the biggest sellers, helped define the classic nature of the Schwinn Company and their innovative products.

Everything you want to know about the Schwinn Whizzers would be enough data to fill an entire book in itself. If you're looking for something worthy of adjectives like classic,

This 1947 Whizzer was born as a result of a joint effort between the Schwinn and Whizzer companies. Prior to that, Whizzer motor kits were installed on many types of bicycles. The Schwinn "WZ" model had thicker spokes, a heavier coil in the spring fork, and a Fore-wheel brake. The vast lore of the Whizzer could fill a book by itself.

cool, unique, and innovative, the Whizzer is it. The Schwinn Whizzer (more accurately the Whizzer-equipped Schwinn) has the style, the features, the age, and the quirkiness to endear itself to just about any classic collector. Other bicycle models may have had names or styles that implied speed or motorization, but the Whizzer actually *had* the motor.

The lore of the Schwinn Whizzer creates some of its mystique. Whizzers were not exclusively Schwinn products. In fact, they were a marriage of two products: Schwinn bicycles and Whizzer motors. The Whizzer Motor Company out of California made some four-stroke gasoline engine kits for use on bicycles during World War II. After the war, the company was sold and moved to Pontiac, Michigan. The then-vice president, Ray Burch, negotiated with Frank W. Schwinn in 1948 to market Schwinns with Whizzer motors. Accounts of that negotiation have probably varied a little, but in the end there was not only an agreement about the motorized bike, but Ray Burch went to work for Schwinn.

Evidently, the Schwinn frames were best suited for the Whizzer motor kits, although there were other early non-Schwinn Whizzers. The strength of the Schwinn cantilever frame was most preferred, though, and was the basis for most of Whizzer's early sales. To cut production costs, Whizzer began making some of its own frames, which were copies of Schwinn's design. Schwinn reacted quickly to protect its patent rights, and shortly after a threatened lawsuit, Frank W. Schwinn and Ray Burch came to some sort of agreeable business arrangement.

Actually, the first Whizzers sold by Schwinn were described in company literature as "Schwinn-Built MOTOR Bicycles." The 1948 model WZ507 had heavy-duty features found on the B-series cycles, such as tubular rims, cantilever frame, expander brakes, and the knee-action spring fork—all features that were even more important on a

The rear fenders of Schwinn Whizzers were notched to accommodate the belt drive system shown here.

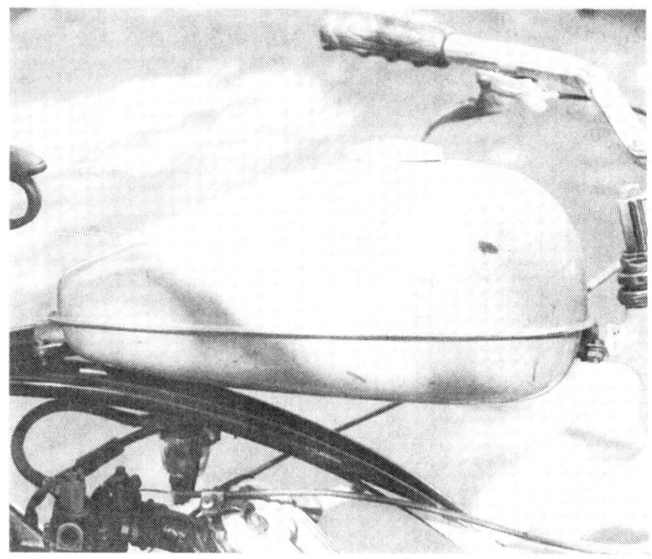

A lot of classic Schwinns had a tank attached to their frames; the Whizzer had the only one that held gasoline.

The single-cylinder, four-cycle Whizzer engine didn't have much horsepower (about 2.5), but fuel mileage was "about five miles to the penny," according to Whizzer advertising.

motorized bicycle. The inspiration for some of those features began during Schwinn's early association with Excelsior and Henderson motorcycles. The Whizzer Company sold Whizzers that had Schwinn frames, and Schwinn sold Schwinn frames that had Whizzer motor kits. There was obviously some sort of blended marketing effort in effect; many of the Whizzer company outlets just happened to be Schwinn retailers.

At any rate, the motorized bicycle market was not growing, but shrinking, and by the late 1950s was not much of a factor. In the meantime, a lot of old Whizzers made a lot of boys and girls very happy, and some cool classics were born along the way. The added mechanical functions inherent to the engine and drive mechanisms make evaluating a vintage Whizzer more challenging than with most old bicycles. There are a lot

Because of the significant classic appeal of the Whizzers, enthusiasts perform meticulous restorations as with the one shown here. The nostalgia for these old relics is so great that new retro Whizzers are now being produced.

The Schwinn Cycle Trucks appeared in the "special" section of the catalog. They were built in a virtually unchanged configuration from 1939 through 1967. The Cycle Truck shown here was built in the early 1950s and has a top tube Schwinn decal from the 1960s, but it looks just like the Cycle Trucks of the 1940s.

of parts and literature available for the Whizzer, however, so help is available. The nostalgia stirred by these gas-powered machines has led to the recent release of a reproduction Whizzer. Do you suppose they had to battle with Schwinn again?

The Schwinn Cycle Truck was one of those inventions that seems like it could have happened a lot sooner. As it was, 1939 was the year Schwinn came out with the versatile delivery bicycle known as the Cycle Truck. This special classic Schwinn had a frame design all of its own, and used a 26-inch rear tire and a 20-inch tire up front. This setup allowed room for the big basket atop the front tire. The weight was not carried by the front fork, though, but rather by the frame, permitting "the Cycle Truck to be steered and balanced the same easy way as an ordinary bicycle," according to Schwinn. The front wheel turned left and right independently from the basket, while the basket and its cargo stayed still.

After its 1939 introduction, the Cycle Truck model stayed in the Schwinn catalogs through 1967. It was sold virtually unchanged for all of those model years; even the two basket size choices were the same in 1967 as they were in 1939 (24 x 16 x 11 inches, or 28 x 22 x 11 inches). In 1939, the color choices were white; ivory or cream with blue stripe; or black, light red, blue, or bright yellow with stripe. By the 1960s, the only color was red. From start to finish, the Cycle Trucks used 2.125-inch balloon tires and had heavy-duty hubs, brakes, spokes, and frames. There was also a metal sign in the tank area that was usually painted with a company's name or logo.

If you crave the thrill of the hunt, then look for a Power Cycle Truck, which was built by Schwinn in 1953 to "meet the demand for low cost speedy retail delivery,"

The Cycle Trucks used a head badge like this one that is peeking through the wires of the basket. The basket dimensions (you could get a small or large one) remained the same throughout Cycle Truck production.

according to dealer propaganda. The same brochure claimed that the Power Cycle Truck, equipped with a Whizzer motor kit, was easy to sell to grocers, hardware stores, beverage dealers, florists, drug stores, and bakeries. Power or not, the Cycle Truck was used by businesses and factories all over the country for many purposes, for many years.

Schwinn sold a few thousand Cycle Trucks per year over the production run, with a spike in sales (about 10,000 annual) during the World War II years. Fuel rationing and truck tire shortages during the war helped increase merchant demand for the Cycle Truck. Fast, economical delivery service was promised with this Schwinn, and merchants were proving it. Schwinn even suggested to its dealers that if the Cycle Trucks were introduced to a local enterprising merchant, the idea would spread and the orders would roll in. They were probably right.

The serial numbers on the Cycle Trucks appear on the lower side of the crank hanger (bottom bracket) through 1951, and at the left rear axle dropout after that. Just about any Cycle Truck is a good find. Since most of

Another bicycle that appeared in the "special" section of the Schwinn catalog was the Run-A-Bout. It was a folding bike with 16-inch wheels, and resembled a Midget Sting-Ray. They were only built in 1968, 1969, and 1970. The 1968 version shown here represents the only year for which whitewalls and a Stik-Shift were available.

them were purchased to use (or abuse), nice originals are rare, but they are worthy of restoration. As with any classic bicycle, certain challenges exist in the restoration of Cycle Trucks. For example, there are many Cycle Truck-only parts used, like the brackets that hold the plywood shelf under the basket. Restoring one of these may require some mechanical *and* carpentry skills.

Hand-operated levers like the one shown here afforded ease of setup, adjustment, and fold-up, without the use of tools.

Another special classic Schwinn was actually grouped with the Sting-Ray models: the Run-A-Bout. This special model was a compact-size, folding bicycle that was advertised as ideal for campers, sportsmen, pilots, yachtsmen, and hunters. It was essentially an obscure product that was just weird enough to be assured of a future cult status. You could set up or fold up this unique bicycle without any tools; special screws and levers were all designed for hand use. Even seat and handlebar adjustments were made without the use of tools, due to the quick-release fittings. It was hard to see just what market Schwinn was after with this one. For example, the Run-A-Bout was advertised as suitable for hunters, but the bike's Gripper Slik rear tire was hardly appropriate for rough terrain.

Most Schwinn tandems after 1962 were called Schwinn Twinns. Exceptions to that were the "Bicycle Built For Two" tandems like the 1963 model shown here. These were only produced in 1963 and 1964, and had an extra top frame bar in the front-rider position.

This 1950 tandem is representative of the post-World War II tandems produced through 1962. They were called tandems up until 1960, when the name Town and Country first appeared on the enclosed chain guards. That practice continued in 1961 and 1962.

Tandems had heavy-duty parts throughout their construction, like this huge tube connecting the two bottom brackets. They also used heavy-gauge spokes and special pieces like the chain tensioner seen here.

The Run-A-Bout was only offered for the 1968, 1969, and 1970 model years, making the current supply very small. This folding Sting-Ray was available in familiar Campus Green and a color borrowed from 10-speed models, Sierra Brown. All of these little bikes had three-speed rear hubs, and the inaugural Run-A-Bout of 1968 could be ordered with a Stik-Shift. They all had 16-inch rims and tires, but the 1968 Run-A-Bout was the only one with whitewalls. If the bike you seek is rare and unique, the Run-A-Bout will certainly fill the bill. It's not one bit practical, and that's part of what makes it a classic.

Schwinn built multi-seat models right from the company's origin. The two-place models, or tandems, were the only models to be mass-marketed, though. The main features that make the tandems special are their heavy-duty parts (e.g., spokes and frame tubes) and special pieces (e.g., rear handlebar clamp and chain tensioner). These special "tandem-only" characteristics increase the interest in these classic bicycles. The very early tandems had no model names, but by the 1950s one was named the Town and Country. These models used a totally enclosed chain guard, another feature unique to them.

Schwinn made a lot of racing tandems, like the 1968 Paramount shown here. The United States team actually rode this particular bike in the 1968 Olympics.

The tandems of the 1950s carried this solid brass badge on the head tube; it's a classic item all by itself.

The last time the Town and Country name was used on a tandem was 1962, and the name coined for the 1963 tandems was "Twinn." The Schwinn Twinn had heavy-duty parts and construction, including a 1–1/2 inch diameter bottom tube. Schwinn claimed that the Twinns were "Sized right for easy, graceful handling—sturdily built for safety."

One promotional tandem, the Bicycle Built For Two, was sold in 1963. There was even a Schwinn record (a vinyl 33–1/3 LP) available for you to buy with the bike. The Bicycle Built For Two had a unique frame with a boys' (high bar) front position, and girls' (low bar) rear position. This feature was a bit male chauvinist in nature, but the women's liberation movement was not that strong at that time.

None of the tandems have the classic clout that the best classic Schwinns do. Like lightweights, they don't have as much style or as many cool features as the popular heavyweights, middleweights, and Sting-Rays. Any Schwinn tandem is still a worthy collector bicycle, however. They are unique in their purpose and a whole lot of fun to ride.

The Town and Country name ended for the tandems after 1962, but it was revived for the 1968 introduction of the three-wheeler. The rear basket with carrying handles was detachable, as evident on this 1970 model.

It's difficult to say why the Town and Country tandem became the Twinn; again, the whims of Schwinn were at play. Schwinn did not discard the name, though, because in 1968 the new adult tri-wheeler was introduced as a Town and Country. The three-wheeled Town and Country was aimed at the older crowd, and had a large basket affixed at the rear. The Town and Country remained in the catalog through 1982, so quite a few were sold. The "trike" is another example of an intriguing Schwinn product that is still plentiful and affordable. Like so many Schwinns, the Town and Country tri-wheeler will never be a top classic, but it will always have classic form and function.

The special classic Schwinns all possess peculiar personas and purposes. Schwinn placed the Run-A-Bout, the Town and Country tandem, the Twinn, and the Town and Country tri-wheeler all under the "Special Models" heading in the dealer catalogs over the years. What they branded as "special" then, seems to be special now, too. Any of these bikes found in good condition are certainly worth preserving, and others in lesser condition are probably worth fixing up. These bikes were designed for recreation and leisure in their day, and they still create as much fun now. They all have a timeless character that is a must for a classic bicycle.

Chapter 7

Lightweight Schwinns

★★½	Paramount
★	Other Lightweight Schwinns

As with the title of Chapter 2 (Antique Schwinns), the title for this chapter does not contain the word *classic*. That's because, like the antiques, the lightweight Schwinn bicycles lack the design and flair of some of the other bikes that have been presented here. For one thing, all of the lightweights except girls' models use simple diamond frames instead of the stylish, early ballooner frames, or the famed cantilever designs; plus, there's not even a *place* for a tank! Nonetheless, this does not minimize the lightweights' durability,

Schwinn lightweights were never able to compete effectively against the imports. This 1961 Traveler typifies the lightweight models that Schwinn tried to market to adults from the 1940s to the 1960s. They were great bikes, but never sold that well, and are not really considered classic Schwinns at this time. The good news: they are currently inexpensive.

Even the Schwinn Paramounts are not among the top classic Schwinns. They are wonderful vintage racing machines and have plenty of value, but their simple diamond-frame design does not appeal to most of us in the classic sense.

rideability, and noteworthy place in Schwinn's history. Also, because of the quality of the lightweights, there are still many remaining today. As supply of the more popular classic Schwinns dwindles and their prices rise, bicycle collectors will migrate toward the plentiful, cheaper lightweights to satisfy their habits. The interest and value in the lightweight models will undoubtedly increase in the future, and only time will tell if the hobbyists will call them classics.

Actually, the lightweight model presence has spanned more decades than any other type of Schwinn. Lightweights were so functional and practical that their existence was mandatory. This practicality kept them from attaining some of the more classic appeal that was accomplished with the equipped balloon-tire, middleweight, and Sting-Ray bicycles that were allowed impractical features. The lightweight models were mainly marketed to adults up to the mid-1960s, but the adult market was never as large as the kid market after the automobile gained popularity.

The very earliest Schwinns were actually lightweight models, but they were not designated as such, because there were no heavyweights or middleweights around yet for comparison. Those early relics are still best described as antiques, though, and the first Schwinns that were actually marketed as lightweights were named the Paramount and the Superior. Many other lightweight models followed over the next few decades, including the Traveler, the Suburban, the

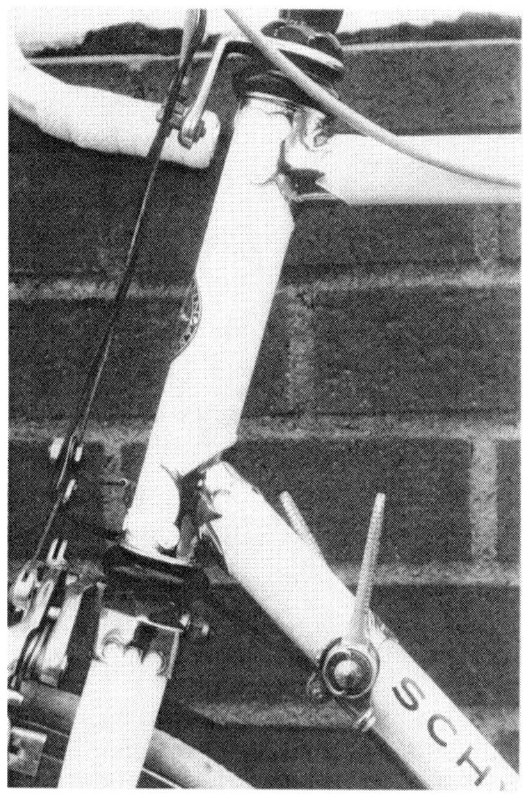

The Paramounts were never a moneymaker for Schwinn. They were all virtually custom made, and had chrome-moly frames with high-quality lugs like the ornate ones shown on the head tube of this 1972 model.

Paramounts were known for their outstanding components, like the precision-engineered Campagnolo crank and chain-ring setup shown here.

Varsity, the Continental, the Collegiate, and the Le Tour, among others.

Among all of those lightweight models, there are many standouts regarding innovation and market impact. Leading the way was the Paramount. The Paramount, which began the genre of bicycles that were designated "lightweights", made its debut in 1938. Development of the bike was a joint effort of Frank W. Schwinn and famous Chicago bicycle maker Emil Wastyn. Schwinn spared no expense in creating the Paramount, and only the finest materials and components were used in its construction. This product philosophy probably helped Schwinn's image, but never helped Schwinn's profits. They could never set a retail price that allowed them to both compete in the market *and* make a profit. The first Paramount (1938) was priced at $75, and some of the final Paramounts (1979) were priced around $1,000.

For sure, the Paramounts were of top quality. The frames were made of the finest chrome molybdenum, seamless drawn, double-butted tubing. The crank was a three-piece cottered type, of racing heritage. All of the components were the finest that Schwinn could hand craft or import from Europe. Yes, the Paramounts were probably the finest bicycles built; they only weighed 20 pounds and were virtually custom built for each customer. But the term "classic" just

The Varsity 10-speed bikes were introduced in 1960 and achieved fair success through the decade. This 1971 model typifies the simple yet durable design of these lightweights (they were a bit heavier than most of the competition).

doesn't define their persona, with their simple diamond frames and lack of extras. Some type of designation like "vintage racer" or "vintage exotic" seems more appropriate for these notable, old bicycles, which definitely generate a lot of interest and hold good value.

The impetus for the Paramount's name choice is pretty easy to figure out. Frank W. Schwinn set out to make an important bike that would be atop the industry. The name Paramount certainly implies that, and so does the model name Superior. The Superior was introduced in 1938, along with the Paramount. The Superior was also a model that lived up to its name, carrying most of the same quality as the Paramount. The seat for the Superior was imitation leather (Paramount seats were leather), it had cheaper hubs than the Paramount, and it cost $20 less than the Paramount in 1938. Both of these bikes were available as racer models (with racing handlebars, pedals, and devoid of fenders or chain guard), or sports-tourist models (with fenders, chain guard, and upright handlebars). When it comes to Schwinn lightweights, the Paramounts and Superiors were then and are now in a class of their own.

Frank W. Schwinn envisioned a country of adults riding lightweight Schwinn bicycles for transportation, health, and pleasure. That was his wish, but it never really happened. In 1940, for example, lightweights accounted for only about five percent of Schwinns sold. To improve this situation, in 1940 Schwinn introduced the New World model, named after the World bicycle that got the company started. The New World was sold at a lower price than the Paramount and the Superior. Again, the New

Schwinn lightweights took many forms over the years; this 1968 Deluxe Breeze is one of those variations, with upright handlebars and a three-speed hub. The saddlebag baskets and generator-powered light were installed by the original dealer.

World was a very plain, practical bicycle with a simple diamond frame.

Hoping to boost sales after World War II, Schwinn introduced more lightweight models and intensified its marketing efforts. Schwinn enlisted popular movie stars of the 1950s to help advertise and endorse new models. (One such celebrity endorser, Ronald Reagan, later became president.) A model introduced in the early 1950s, the World Traveler, was designed to compete directly with the imports. Ad copy for this model proclaimed, "Schwinn lightweights feel light as a feather and ride like the breeze! And they're American made, too!" The difficulty in gaining ground on the imports, though, was that the deluge of bikes from France and England were sold at a cheaper price. Even through the 1950s, lightweights never accounted for more than 10 percent of all Schwinn bicycles sold.

During the 1950s, Schwinn lightweights were built in both boys' and girls' (or men's and ladies') versions. The Paramount was still paramount, but more affordable models were sold with names like Traveler, Sports, Varsity (not the later, more popular model), and Racer. These bikes were all quality machines, but lacked kid appeal. The adults were not buying that many bikes, and the European competition was fierce, so even with new models and lots of advertising, Schwinn lightweights took a back seat to the rest of the model offerings.

By 1960, thanks to the presence of the imports and a concerted advertising effort by Schwinn, American youth were noticing the lightweights for the first time. Multi-speed derailleur-equipped bikes had been found all over Europe since 1910, and were

Many names and features were used on lightweight and 10-speed Schwinn bicycles. This 1977 Caliente has a unique freewheeling front sprocket that rotates while you coast to make shifting gears easier.

finally beginning to appear in California. As in the case of the muscle-bike movement, dealers alerted Schwinn to this latest trend. Again, it was Al Fritz who ran with the idea and quickly brought the 10-speed Continental model to market in 1960. Orders for the Continental came quickly.

The same year the Continental was introduced, the moderately priced eight-speed Varsity was introduced. The Varsity name was revived from the 1950s lightweight of the same name. The Varsity became a 10-speed in 1961, and it was in place at a perfect time for the upcoming bicycle boom. Not only were the 10-speed models catching on, but by the mid-1960s the middleweights and Sting-Rays were selling well, too. The Varsity stayed around through the mid-1980s, when Schwinn was losing its direction and missing out on the BMX and mountain-bike movements.

The Varsity models introduced the American masses to derailleur bikes, and that distinction gives them a bit more classic status than the rest of the lightweights. They also arrived in the showrooms with eye-popping colors like yellow, orange, and lime green, affording them another distinction over their more boring lightweight counterparts. If you think that the Varsity is a classic, now is the time to buy, because they are currently both plentiful and inexpensive.

Typically, models with other names and features spun off of the popular Varsity. The Collegiate model, which was no doubt

Schwinn Collegiate lightweights, such as this one, were apparently aimed at the college crowd. Boys' and girls' (shown) models were sold throughout the 1960s and 1970s.

aimed at the college market, came out for sale in 1964, and could be ordered with a one-, two-, three-, or five-speed setup. Another bike with an obvious name image was the Racer. By 1970, a Suburban model with upright handlebars was in the mix, and a girls- (or ladies-) only Breeze was another popular lightweight of this period. The derailleur models were now using a 27-inch tire with a 1-1/4 inch width. The one-, two-, and three-speed lightweights were still equipped with 26 by 1-3/8-inch tires. The differences helped to create two designations for these bikes: lightweight and 10-speed.

Through the 1970s and 1980s, there were many other lightweights in the Schwinn catalog, with names such as Super Sport, Sprint, Sierra, Caliente, and Le Tour. The Le Tour was Schwinn's first Japanese-built bicycle. In the collector hobby, none of these lightweights are really considered true classics. They are, however, quality bikes with a character and a history that warrants notice. They are also pretty low on the cost scale, with the exception of old Paramounts. Maybe now is the time to find them, and hold them until the interest and value rises. You can even enjoy riding them while you wait!

Chapter 8

Contemporary Classic Schwinns

★★½	Cruisers
★½	Reproduction Sting-Rays
★★★	Factory Reproduction Phantom

Are you into retro? An interest in retro refers to a celebration of the past. The classic bicycles of Schwinn's past are reason for celebration, and the current retro movement proves it. Throughout the 1980s and 1990s, Schwinn celebrated the 1950s and 1960s via its nostalgic Cruisers and other reproductions. Whenever copies of classic original bicycles go to market, it certainly solidifies the classic status of the originals. The recent Cruiser line of Schwinn bicycles, reproduction Sting-Rays, and the 1995 Centennial reproduction Black

The purchasers of the Schwinn Company after its 1993 bankruptcy, the Scott Sports Group, had a sense of nostalgia and retro heritage. They not only continued with Schwinn's Cruiser line, but also added some Phantom-inspired accessories like the tank, fenders, rear carrier, and spring fork. The influence of the past is obvious on this 1997 Cruiser Deluxe.

The Cruiser Super Seven shown here is actually a 2001 model. It incorporates a state-of-the-art, internal shifting seven-speed hub into a classic bicycle design. The Schwinn Company changed hands again in late 2001, so the future of retro products remains to be seen.

Phantoms are not really classics now, but they are certainly copies of classics. Time will tell if they will be looked upon as true classic bicycles in the future.

Schwinn introduced a new Cruiser model in 1980. It was a blend of heavyweight and middleweight design. At the time of the Cruiser's introduction, Schwinn's middleweight line was down to a model that was hardly selling anymore: the Typhoon. The first Cruisers were fender-less, cantilever frame bicycles equipped with soft seats and balloon tires. That's right, Schwinn dragged out the balloon tires again, and the Cruisers all sported the old 2.125-inch tires. These tires were called "studded," which meant that they had a knobby-type tread. The Cruisers had totally replaced the middleweight class by 1983, when both boys' and girls' Cruisers were offered.

In 1982, 20-inch and 24-inch boys' Cruisers appeared in the catalog. The smaller versions typically sold in smaller numbers, making them quite rare now. The 20-year history of the Cruiser bikes began with a fairly bare-bones model. The Cruisers then evolved through a period in which they started getting accessories such as fenders,

tanks, and racks. Finally, they reached a point where the latest technology was blended into their designs. This process followed a typical pattern, where a basic model is offered to start, and each succeeding model becomes "new and improved."

By the year 2000, there were five Cruisers in the Schwinn catalog, all with a mix of classic

Left: They are good adaptations of classic bicycles, but the foreign-manufactured classic cruisers (one model is even named Classic Cruiser) will not attain the classic status of the Chicago-built originals.

Below: This 1995 Black Phantom is a reproduction of a circa-1950 model. In 1995, the new owners of Schwinn, the Scott Sports Group, faithfully reconstructed several thousand of these. The time and expense of the undertaking gave validation to the classic stature of the original Phantoms.

Classic features tend to have a timeless appeal. When the reproduction Phantoms came out in 1995, the Phantom tank, the streamlined Fenderlite, the spring fork, and the Typhoon Cord whitewalls all looked just as good as they did in 1949.

Even detail items like the "Schwinn Approved" embossing on the leather Phantom seat were included on the reproductions, and they were built in the United States.

features and new technology. The Cruiser Deluxe Seven was equipped with a Phantom-style tank, a rack, a headlight, and a spring fork, juxtaposed with modern alloy rims and an internal-shifting seven-speed rear hub. You make the gear changes with a state-of-the-art twist-grip shifter. That's quite a mixture of old and new, and it's an unusual blend like this that can create a future classic. Evidently, Schwinn had an opinion about the classic status of these bikes right off the bat, since they offered a model called a Cruiser Classic in 1997; another model appearing in the 2000 product brochure was named the Cruiser Classic Four. The Classic Four was based on a cantilever frame, and had a four-speed internal- shifting hub. Evidently, the philosophy for making this bicycle a classic was as simple as naming it that way. It's true that the Cruisers were produced overseas, and that they are not that old yet, but in the future they will be considered classics by many people, but will never

One feature that identified the 1995 reproduction Black Phantoms was the embossed coaster brake arm. It read, "Schwinn 1895-1995 Centennial," commemorating the 100-year anniversary of Schwinn. These Black Phantom reproductions are probably bargains now, as they are selling for less than their original $3,000 price.

be as popular as the Chicago-built bikes. The recent sale of the Schwinn brand name rights to Pacific Cycles (maker of the Mongoose bikes) leaves the future production of these retro bikes uncertain. It is not likely that the current run of nostalgic bicycles will continue, which will classify their production as limited and place them a step closer to having classic status.

The first sale of the Schwinn Company (to the Scott Sports Group) carried quite a bit of nostalgic heritage with it. This sentiment was evident when the new Schwinn Company decided to celebrate the 100-year history of Schwinn with a re-creation of the legendary 1949 Black Phantom. This was not an ordinary reproduction; it was to be a near-exact copy, built using original plans and specifications. The result was a 1995 Centennial Edition Black Phantom that was hard to tell from an original one. All of the neat features such as the horn-tank, headlight, taillight, rack, pinstriping, pedals, reflectors, and leather seat, looked like new old stock (unused vintage parts). One identifying feature was the imprint on the coaster brake arm, "Schwinn 1895-1995 Centennial." The reproduction Black Phantoms were expensive (around $3,000.00), and Schwinn had a hard time selling them. The most popular

In the late 1990s Schwinn commissioned the Asian production of a Sting-Ray remake. Some collectors shun these copies, but others proudly display them right next to the old bicycles. As evidenced by this 1999 model, they *look* like Sting-Rays, and it *says* Sting-Ray on the chain guard, so they must *be* Sting-Rays.

These are Sting-Rays all right, right down to the reproduction Slik tire; unfortunately, they are not as classic or as collectible as the originals.

The legend of an original Grape Krate has never been confirmed. There is no question that this 1999 reproduction version exists, however, as proven by the photo. The paint is purple, and it certainly has the classic Krate heritage.

If you buy a retro Cruiser or reproduction Sting-Ray now, you will probably see the value drop a bit before it goes back up. Given some time, though, these bikes will garner increased interest and value, and they can still be found brand new today.

story is that they were going to produce about 5,000 copies, but with the trouble they had selling them, only about 3,000 frames became Black Phantoms, and the rest were made into Green and Red Phantoms. As time passes, these bikes will be considered classics, because of the story that goes with them and their limited run.

Besides the Cruisers and the Phantoms, Schwinn also sold some reproduction Sting-Rays in the late 1990s. These were not the painstakingly crafted jewels that the Phantoms were, as the new Sting-Rays were mass-produced in China and Taiwan. Nevertheless, they look like Sting-Rays, and they are called Sting-Rays, so they must be Sting-Rays. Any retro movement involving Schwinn bicycles simply must include this impractical yet fun model from the past.

Schwinn woke the childhood memories of many people with the reintroduction of certain Sting-Ray models in 1998. The new

Asian-built reproduction bicycles were close copies of the fun and stylish little bike that debuted in 1963. The first offerings mimicked the early, basic Sting-Ray with a cantilever frame and no fenders. The new Sting-Ray still had a vinyl-covered banana seat, high-rise handlebars, and a Slik rear tire, just like the early ones. Some diehard purists rejected the new copy, while other collectors purchased the new versions to occupy space right next to their original ones. The reproductions were available with a paint finish of either blue or yellow.

Throughout the history of Schwinn, unequipped bicycle model introductions were usually followed with equipped model introductions. This was the same philosophy in 1999, when Schwinn followed up the reproduction Sting-Rays with reproduction Sting-Ray Krates. The two Krates chosen for the honor were the top two sellers of the past: the Orange Krate and the Apple Krate. The reproduction models were copied quite faithfully, and included most of the original features. Unfortunately, one of the most interesting original items, the bar-mounted Stik-Shift, could not be used on the new Krates. The consumer product watchdogs didn't like it; they outlawed it in 1974, and were not about to change their minds in today's litigious environment.

The new Krates, like the Sting-Rays, were available only with a single-speed coaster brake hub. The early Krates were offered with a coaster brake too, but the appeal of the five-speed shifter made coaster brake models pretty scarce. The reproduction Krates were supposedly copies of 1972 models, and the way they were outfitted helped recapture the original classic appeal. The new models came with color-keyed, racing-striped, metallic-vinyl banana seats; chrome fenders; spring fork; white-lettered Slik; seat spring-shocks; and a 16-inch front tire. Overall, the new Krates had a lot of the cool factor pioneered by their older counterparts. As a 2000 brochure describes, "Like holding a baby, or walking a puppy, this is a fantastic way to meet members of the opposite sex."

The "new" Schwinn was not quite finished making new bikes yet. To pay homage to the rumors of the legendary Grape Krate, Schwinn decided to build one. So in 1999, they added one more newly fashioned Krate to the line. The Grape Krate was like the other Krates, but it was painted a beautiful metallic purple, and sported a matching purple seat and handgrips. The elusive Grape Krate was now a reality; not a vintage original, but pretty cool anyway.

Reproduction Schwinn bicycles (Phantoms and Sting-Rays) and vintage-inspired Cruisers can be categorized as "neo-classics," or classics of the future. Since there is already collector interest in these models, there is little doubt that a large group of followers will covet them in the years to come. They all emulate and celebrate the cantilever frame, one of the best achievements of Schwinn, and absolutely one of the main features responsible for the company's success. Excellent original bikes will always outvalue these copies, but the presence of these new models allows more people to appreciate and enjoy the retro movement. There can be no dispute that the reproductions are close copies of the originals, and the 1995 Black Phantoms are nearly duplicates. These models are all bargains in the current market. Explore what's out there!

Chapter 9

Other Schwinns of Interest

★★½	Bantam
★	BMX bicycles
★	Mountain bikes

No matter how many Schwinn models you talk about, it seems there are always some left over. So far, we've looked at antiques, heavyweights, middleweights, lightweights, Sting-Rays, special models, and current models. That look represents a lot of bikes, but there are many more. Since just about any Schwinn in good condition will be of interest to someone at some time, the hobby of collecting Schwinn bicycles will endure. Like some of the girls' bikes, lightweights, and contemporary models, there are other models that are

The Schwinn Bantams, like this 1967 bike, should qualify as classic Schwinns due to longevity alone. They were around from the 1950s through the 1980s. These 20-inch bikes have a classic look and a classic feature: They are "convertibles," and change from boys' bikes to girls' bikes by moving or removing the top bar.

The top bar may be swung down to a clamp, or removed completely to change the Bantam from a boy's bike to a girls' bike, as shown here.

easy to find now and in good supply. These bikes are inexpensive, and because demand for them in the future will surely rise, they are a good value today.

The middleweight Schwinns did not fully disappear when production of the Typhoon and Hollywood models ceased in 1982. The Bantam was there to fill the void through 1985. Actually, the original Bantam entered the model listings in 1950 and only lasted through 1953. That very first Bantam had 16-inch rims with 2.125-inch balloon tires, and came with or without Cycle-Aids (training wheels). The most unique feature of the Bantam right from the start was its "convertible" designation. That's right, it was a convertible because it could be converted from a boys' bike to a girls' bike and vice versa. You could remove (or swing down) the top frame bar of the Bantam, changing its gender bias. That way, this juvenile bicycle could then pass down from brother to sister, or the other way around, as the older child grew out of it. It seems like a marketing gimmick, but those quirky gimmicks help make classics.

The Bantam came back in 1960 as a middleweight, and was again listed in the catalog as a convertible bicycle, with or without Cycle-Aids. The middleweight edition used 20-inch rims with 1-3/4 inch tires. Even if the convertible top bar was a gimmick, the Bantam held a spot in the lineup for another 25 years. The middleweight Bantams up through around 1969 typically have more of a classic (vintage) look than the later ones. Starting with 1970, the serial numbers moved from the left rear dropout to the head tube, and additional reflectors were added to the pedals, spokes, seat, and handlebars. The rear fender reflector got huge and rectangular, and was mounted with two studs, as opposed to the earlier single-stud, round reflector. The Bantams were all basic coaster brake models, although some did come with whitewall tires.

If you find a balloon Bantam (1950-1953), you will have a prized piece; if you find a middleweight Bantam, you'll have a nifty bicycle worth hanging on to. Regardless of age, any bicycle that has a changeable boy/girl nature is some sort of classic.

Following Schwinn's big list of classic heavyweight balloon bicycles, the middleweight, Sting-Ray, lightweight, and special models were all market successes within the boom years of 1955-1975. The only classic aspect of Schwinn's upcoming foray into the off-road bicycle market was that it was a classic example of too little, too late. While good timing had been with Schwinn in the past, the company was behind the competition in its

BMX and mountain bike offerings. There had always been pockets of off-road bicycle use, but signs that more riders were heading to the hills began in the mid-1970s. New names for the hobby/sport of off-road cycling were coined about this same time: BMX (Bicycle Motocross) and mountain biking. BMX cycling emulated motorcycle motocross on 20-inch bikes, and mountain biking simply involved riding full-size balloon-tire bikes on dirt in the hills.

With new names for their activities, millions of participants were entering what would become the next two phenomena in bicycling. Whether by luck or wisdom, there were entrepreneurs other than Schwinn that got the timing right for the burgeoning markets of BMX and mountain bicycles. Schwinn had the clout to put forth a major effort in this field, but they did not, and other smaller companies excelled. Mountain bike makers like Trek and BMX specialists like Mongoose were introducing the latest technology in their fields at that time. Schwinn did not react quickly or very seriously to these markets, and the market stronghold of the competition could not be broken. This failure was a big factor in the unraveling at Schwinn.

Even though it was a delayed, weak response, Schwinn did eventually produce some models for these markets. The BMX market opened up first, and when Schwinn fielded its first BMX model in 1977, others had already taken the lead, namely Skip Hess, who founded the Mongoose Bicycle

BMX bikes like this 1983 Thrasher were good, but Schwinn got into the game too late. As far as classics, BMX bikes don't have that much appeal. Notice that the frame is a squashed diamond design.

Once they got rolling, Schwinn had many BMX models. This 1984 Gremlin was for the small BMX rider, because it only had 16-inch wheels.

Company. Ironically, the company that markets Mongoose bicycles (Pacifica LLC) now owns Schwinn. The first BMX model Schwinn produced, the 20-inch Scrambler, was actually classified as a Sting-Ray in the catalog; it still had a banana seat. Schwinn was operating under old philosophies, which was reasonable, given the successes of the past. They even listed a 16-inch Mini Scrambler in the 1977 catalog, proving their naiveté in the marketplace. What didn't quite register with Schwinn was that serious riders wanted their bikes to have the latest technology, like chrome-moly frames outfitted with lightweight running gear.

The independent companies were making headway, and Schwinn was only partially interested. Besides simply resting on past laurels, Schwinn top management was also concerned with BMX liability issues. By 1978, "Motocross" did at least have its own heading in the Schwinn catalog. The models for 1978 were the Scrambler, the Competition Scrambler, the Mag Scrambler (with mag as opposed to spoke wheels), and the Mini-Scrambler. In addition to red or blue paint, you could get a Scrambler with a chrome frame, too.

Something new for Schwinn was that their BMX bikes were generally cheaper than the competition's so far. This should have been another signal to Schwinn; their bikes had never been considered inexpensive. To make the BMX bike that the market wanted would cost more money. In 1979, this message was finally getting through, and Schwinn started selling Team Schwinn MX frames that were more expensive than the standard complete bikes. This way, customers could get a state-of-the-art frame, and add their own high-tech components (which Schwinn didn't have). Schwinn even

There may have been many Schwinn BMX models, but the direction Schwinn was aiming for was unclear. This 1985 girls' Predator came with white tires that weren't too practical for dirt.

began sponsoring racing teams at this time. Finally Schwinn was headed in the right direction, but they had simply waited too long to capture a major share of the market.

For 1980, there were over a dozen motocross model variations listed in Schwinn's catalog, including the Phantom Scrambler and the Sting. In 1981, names like Predator and Thrasher joined the BMX group. Up through 1985, you'd find the Sting, the Competition, the Predator, the Scrambler, the Phantom, and the Thrasher (in descending order of price) in the Schwinn showrooms.

Another national mood change must have occurred in the mid-1980s. At least the BMX names Schwinn used were changing. In 1985, model names like Black Shadow, Streetwise, Qualifier, Aerostar, and Gremlin made the lineup. In 1986 the Freeform and the Quarterflash were added to the mix. For 1987, all of the Schwinn BMX models were called Predators. There was now a model and a sub-model, namely Predator Freeform, Predator Quarterflash, Predator Aerostar, and Predator Gremlin. Available colors now had names like Neon Rose, Wild Cherry, Crucial Grape, Ice Mint, and Intense Blue.

As previously mentioned, none of the Schwinn BMX bicycles are very high on the classic list, and the later models simply don't have enough age to warrant much classic consideration yet. Undoubtedly, however, select models from the preceding text are of interest right now, like the early Scrambler. Given some more time, these earlier bikes will be of greater interest, and the later bikes will be of some interest.

Between the two market phenomena, BMX and mountain bikes, Schwinn probably did a better job with the BMX segment. The bad news is that the mountain bike trend proved to be the biggest bicycle movement ever. Schwinn would not have needed to worry about its marginal BMX market share if it had pioneered the mountain bike phenomenon. Instead, Schwinn let newcomers like Trek, Ross, and Specialized dominate the field. This new segment would become over three-fourths of the total bicycle market, partly because these bikes were purchased for both child *and* adult riders.

About the time that these other startup bicycle makers were innovating, the closest thing Schwinn had to a mountain bike was the Cruiser model in 1980 and 1981. Schwinn finally added a category for "all-terrain" bicycles for the 1982 lineup. Refusing to shed its past, Schwinn named its first mountain bike the King-Sting. The Sidewinder was introduced that same year. Those are probably the nearest things to classic Schwinn mountain bikes currently available. The next Schwinn mountain bikes were Asian-built, and probably better bikes, but their foreign manufacture and later production will hold them low on the classic list for now. These imported models came out in 1983 and were called the Sierra and High Sierra. In 1984, the Mesa Runner was added, followed in 1985 by the Mirada and the Cimarron (back to those car names again).

The only thing worse than being late for the BMX phenomenon was being late for the mountain bike market fury. Schwinn made some pretty good mass-market mountain bikes, like this 1995 Frontier; they also built the high-tech Homegrown series of mountain bikes in the mid-1990s. But it was too little, too late, as other makers dominated this market.

In 1986, there was a telling scenario in the Schwinn catalog: They listed 30 Cruiser models, and only five all-terrain models. The damage was done. Schwinn's entry was too late, too little, and somewhat misguided. Schwinn didn't even call these all-terrain models mountain bikes until the 1989 catalog listing. At this same time, Schwinn was struggling with supply, cost, and labor problems of outside suppliers and within their own plant. In the early 1990s, the Frontier line of mountain bikes wasn't selling that badly, but the manufacturing problems negated profits. Bankruptcy was imminent.

Some of the best picks for future classic Schwinns might be the "Homegrown" line of mountain bikes introduced in 1996 by the Scott Sports Group, the new owners of Schwinn. In an attempt at damage control, Schwinn moved its headquarters to Boulder, Colorado, which was one of the birthplaces of mountain biking. They built an off-road testing facility and hired engineers who were mountain bikers to develop a new line of state-of-the-art bikes. They were diligent in their quest, and turned out some wonderful products. Unfortunately, recapturing a market dominated by others was not to be. If you can find a Homegrown suspension model, you will have something that should be better than money in the bank.

It was stated earlier that any Schwinn in good condition will be worth something to somebody some day, so there are a lot of models from which to choose. If you have room, you can hardly go wrong by trying to find some of those nice Schwinn bicycles that are biding time until the world regards them as classics.

Serial Number Guide

The serial numbers for Schwinns, unlike most other brands, have traceable roots. Unfortunately, a factory fire destroyed the records prior to 1948, but we can make some sense out of the numbers used after that. The serial numbers were stamped on the underside of the bottom bracket (crank hanger tube) on all Schwinns up until 1952. During that year, the location for the serial number stampings was moved to the left rear axle dropout. The numbers were stamped on the frame near the dropout until 1970. Serial numbers for 1970 models appear in one of two places, because partway through that year Schwinn began stamping the serial numbers on the head tube, below the head badge. One exception to this is that the Paramount series kept the number at the rear dropout through the 1970s. Some of the Asian-built Schwinns of the 1980s had numbers under the bottom bracket again, but they are not easily traceable.

Most Schwinn serial numbers actually contain letters *and* numbers. In its use of letters, Schwinn did not use the "I" or the "O," so as to avoid confusion with the numbers one and zero. Depending on the vintage of the bicycle on which they appear, the letters and numbers mean different things.

Generally, the 1948-1957 numbers have no pattern, and you must refer to a reference list to determine vintage for this period. For example, a serial number E147986 is found in the listings to be a 1948 model. Stampings from 1958 to 1964 start with one letter followed by six digits. For these years, the letter indicates the month (A=January, B=February, etc., skipping "I") and the first numeral indicates the year (8=1958, 9=1959, etc.). A serial number D132101 is from April 1961. Schwinns from 1965 on have stampings beginning with two letters followed by six digits, where the first letter indicates the month, and the second letter indicates the year, of the frame. A serial number BB57760 designates February 1966.The way the two-letter code works for the 1965 and newer models is as follows: The first letter (skipping "I") coincides with the month: A=January, B=February, C=March, D=April, E=May, F=June, G=July, H=August, J=September, K=October, L=November, and M=December (the month codes are the same for the 1958-1964 models). The second letter (skipping "I" and "O") coincides with the year: A=1965, B=1966, C=1967, D=1968, E=1969, F=1970, G=1971, H=1972, J=1973, K=1974, L=1975, M=1976, N=1977, P=1978, Q=1979, R=1980, S=1981, and T=1982. Another example is that serial number MD41177 was stamped in December of 1968.

Some of the serial numbers with one letter and six digits on earlier bikes fall into the same pattern as the later 1958-1964 numbers. In those cases, the era of the bicycle must be determined by its classification (heavyweight or middleweight, for example) before decoding the number. Reading the preceding chapters of this book will help you figure that out. The following is a list of the serial numbers used that have no built-in code:
CT=Cycle Truck; WZ, S-10=Whizzer; No model codes after 1951

1948
C50000 - C50920
C50951 - C51138
D92598 - D94799
E01032 - E67000
E067001 - E083213
E088017 - E175256
E096521 - E096837
E175522 - E262103
11001WZ - 13398 WZ
1 S-10 - 3447 S-10 (24-inch)

1949
F000100 - F309647
F321358 - F364549
G000100 - G003166
T001000 - T001217 (tandem)
S312850 - S321357
F160598 CT - F163107 CT
5000 WZ - 7408 WZ
3825 S-10 - 5896 S-10

1950
G003167 - G294890
G310130 - G318061
G335123 - G343221
G355966 - G531230
G164355 CT - G165580 CT
5987 S-10 - 6244 S-10
T002347 - T003035 (tandem)
H000001 - H000666
Z294891 - Z355695

1951
H000667 - H437160
H166581 CT - H167354 CT
H272629 CT - H273272 CT
6657 WZ - 7738 WZ
7739 S-10 - 8110 S-10
A01370 - A87593 (new number location at left rear dropout appears on 1952 models)

1952	1956
A87594 - A97867	U57805 - U99999
B00001 - B99999	V00001 - V99999
C00001 - C99999	W00001 - W93942
D00001 - D66447	L00001 - L99999
E00001 - E99999	M03564 - M25000
F00001 - F00000	N25164 - N99999
G00001 - G44000	P00001 - P25622
	R25623 - R38318
1953	
H60001 - H99999	**1957**
J00001 - J99999	B18549 - B99999
K00001 - K99999	C00001 - C99999
A00001 - A99999	D00001 - D24842
B00001 - B99999	R41605 - R161241
C00001 - C99999	S01400 - S47570
D00001 - D20266	7D05700 - 7D49811
	7D24843 - 7D75700
1954	7E0001 - 7E9999
L00001 - L99999	7F0001 - 7F10609
M00001 - M99999	
N00001 - N99999	**1958**
P00001 - P17600	8F10685 - 8F99999
	8G00001 - 8G08079
1955	8L00001 - 8L39400
P17601 - P99999	
R01452 - R99999	
S00001 - S99999	
T00001 - T99999	
U00001 - U56286	

After March 1958, the system described previously took effect. For the next period (through 1964) the beginning letter (like "H" in H811113) designates the month, and the first number ("8" in the example) designates the year. The system (previously described) that placed two letters at the beginning of the serial number began in 1965.

Lengthy day-by-day serial number listings have been printed, to help determine the actual day of the frame stamping. Some Schwinn dealers have this list, and it can often be found at Internet auctions or other Web sites. Space requirements prohibit showing that complete listing here.

Individual model production numbers for Schwinns do not exist.

When the Sting-Ray model was introduced in 1963–1/2 selling 10,000 units of any one model was considered very good. The Sting-Rays exceeded that number in the first half-year. This indicates that any given model probably fell into the 5,000 to 10,000 annual unit sales range. However, this was when total annual Schwinn sales were over a half-million units; prior to that, individual model sales were most likely in the 1,000 to 5,000 unit range. Total annual production figures have been published, and they are:

1932-17,152; 1933-46,090; 1934-86,986; 1935-107,217; 1936-201,442; 1937-168,657; 1938-121,720; 1939-189,907; 1940-224,995; 1941-346,487; 1942-112,859; 1943-16,385; 1944-18,929; 1945-98,185; 1946-302,071; 1947-486,793; 1948-602,408; 1949-352,302; 1950-510,019; 1951-466,849; 1952-478,838; 1953-501,379; 1954-355,790; 1955-413,355; 1956-454,933; 1957-439,482; 1958-451,158 1959-546,238; 1960-514,724; 1961-471,506; 1962-528,721; 1963-655,693; 1964-849,818; 1965-876,608.

For the next decade, annual sales hovered around one million units, and hit a new high of 1.2 million units in 1971, and an all-time high of 1.5 million units in 1974. The brisk sales of the middleweights, ten-speeds, and Sting-Rays accounted for Schwinn's success during this era. If this success had continued during the BMX and mountain bike period, we would probably see a different Schwinn company today. But alas, it was not meant to be, as sales were headed downward.

The new ownership of Schwinn (Pacifica LLC) is experienced in the bicycle market, so it's possible that the Schwinn name will reach new heights. Only time will tell.

Bibliography and Resources

Arnold, Schwinn & Co. *50 Years of Schwinn-Built Bicycles*. Chicago: Arnold, Schwinn & Co., 1945

Fried, Liz. *Schwinn Sting-Ray*. Osceola, WI: Motorbooks International, 1997.

Pridmore, Jay, and Jim Hurd. *Schwinn Bicycles*. Osceola, WI: Motorbooks International, 1996.

Additionally, countless Schwinn advertisements, retail sales brochures, dealer support literature, dealer catalogs, Schwinn Reporters, and other paper products were studied during the research for this book.

All of the preceding documents are good resources for information on the classic Schwinn topic; here are some others:

Vintage *American Bicyclist and Motorcyclist* magazines.

Schwinn Web Page:
http://www.schwinn.com
Heritage Timeline and Classic forums

National Bicycle History Archive of America
Santa Ana, California
http://members.aol.com/oldbicycle/

Dave's Vintage Bicycles
Spokane, Washington
http://www.nostalgic.net

Columbia Cycle Classics
Spokane, Washington
http://www.columbiacycle.com

Vintage Cycle Supply
West Linn, Oregon
http://www.vintagecyclesupply.com

Hyper-Formance (Sting-Rays)
Chandler, Arizona
http://www.hyper-formance.com

Bobcycles Restorations
Torrance, California
E-mail: bobcycles@aol.com

The Classic and Antique Bicycle Exchange
Dalworthington, Texas
http://thecabe.com

Index

CPSIA information can be obtained at www.ICGtesting.com
Printed in the USA
BVOW061133070713

325266BV00005B/18/P